TRUST
FACTOR

The Science of Creating

High-Performance Companies

PAUL J. ZAK

AMACOM

American Management Association

New York • Atlanta • Brussels • Chicago • Mexico City • San Francisco
Shanghai • Tokyo • Toronto • Washington, D.C.

American Management Association: www.amanet.org
This publication is designed to provide accurate and authoritative information in regard to the subject matter covered. It is sold with the understanding that the publisher is not engaged in rendering legal, accounting, or other professional service. If legal advice or other expert assistance is required, the services of a competent professional person should be sought.

LIBRARY OF CONGRESS CATALOGING-IN-PUBLICATION DATA
Names: Zak, Paul J., author.
Title: The trust factor : the science of creating high-performance companies / Paul J. Zak.
Description: New York, NY : AMACOM, [2017]
Identifiers: LCCN 2016036854 (print) | LCCN 2016046864 (ebook)
| ISBN 9780814437667 (hardcover) | ISBN 9780814437674 (ebook)
Subjects: LCSH: Corporate culture. | Trust. | Performance. | Organizational effectiveness. | Organizational behavior. Classification: LCC HD58.7 .Z347
    2017 (print) | LCC HD58.7 (ebook) | DDC658.3/12—dc23
LC record available at https://lccn.loc.gov/2016036854

10 9 8 7 6 5 4 3 2 1

33614057802554

To Mary Beth McEuen, who first convinced me that trust is vital in organizations. Thank you for your trust and friendship.

Contents

Introduction

Arriving in Malke, a remote village of 1,000 people in Papua New Guinea, I had only three days to run the first-ever organizational culture experiment in a rain forest, so I had to get my equipment working. While experiments I ran in my laboratory and in companies in the United States had shown that a culture of trust generates high performance, testing members of an isolated tribe would help me determine if trust improves performance everywhere. Adding to the pressure of doing neuroscience in the rain forest, NHK TV from Japan would be filming the experiment.

Naturally, the experiment gods had other ideas.

Malke has no electricity or running water, so I brought all the supplies I would need: a suitcase full of sterile needles, blood-collection tubes, latex gloves, and a small centrifuge—items that shocked New Guinean customs agents despite my government permit. Waiting for me in the capital, Port Moresby, was a rented generator to run the centrifuge and liquid nitrogen flown in from Japan that I needed to freeze blood samples so I could get them back to my California lab.

A small plane took me to the Western Highlands; then a four-wheel-drive transported me over barely passable mud tracks to Malke. I unloaded my gear, built a serviceable medical hut, and started testing the equipment. The centrifuge made a burning smell that I traced to a buggy voltage regulator, and the liquid nitrogen that I was promised would last a week had evaporated. This deep in the jungle, the markets I could reach sold basic foods and recycled everything else.

My lifeline was Digicel. This Irish-owned, Jamaica-based, low-cost mobile-phone provider allowed me to call liquid nitrogen suppliers from Australia to Japan from 7,000 feet above sea level. So I sat on the grass and started making calls, hoping I could cajole some supplier to make a long-distance delivery. I was agitated and defeated.

Then the villagers began to sit down beside me. After 20 minutes, 30 or 40 people had crowded around, and I put away my phone. The children started holding my hands and smiling. I made faces at them, and we all laughed. The village chief, Edward, came over and put his hands on my shoulders and said, "Hi-oh," the New Guinean pidgin greeting. I said, "Hi-oh" back. Within an hour, I was being treated like a member of the village. The Malkeans welcomed me into their thatched-roof houses and into the outbuildings where the men practiced the rituals of their ancestors. As I relaxed into their hospitality, my problems slipped away.

While the data I would collect were fascinating, my experience in the rain forest was life-changing. I was warmly welcomed into an organization with people to whom I could barely communicate. What made them trust me, and me them?

We humans have been "doing" organizations for perhaps a million years, since our ancestors formed tribes to bring down large prey and jointly care for children. We are exquisitely good organizational men and women. Yet we still struggle to create cultures that are safe, engaging, productive, and innovative. Cultures are the way social creatures transmit information about how we do things and the values we hold sacred. Culture has a powerful effect on human behavior, including behavior at work.

People create cultures, join cultures, and change cultures, yet most of this is done unintentionally, so we are unaware we are doing it. In order to understand how organizational culture affects performance at work and in life, a decade ago I started measuring brain activity from people while they worked.

One reason for our culture blindness at work is that we instinctively create culture. Because it arises without effort, we hardly notice it. Anthropologists measure the attributes of cultures through observation, but the approach my research team has taken is different.[1] As neuroscientists, we asked if culture could be designed for high engagement based on our knowledge of the social brain. Recent findings in social neuroscience—a number of them from my lab—have provided fresh insights into why some organizations achieve high performance while others stumble. We call this approach to organizational design neuromanagement.[2] This book reports a decade's worth of testing and refinements of these implications, including field experiments in businesses and my consulting work for for-profit companies, nonprofits, and government agencies.

Leaders of organizations have been allergic to measuring culture for a variety of reasons, foremost among them because managing people has been seen as an art, not a science. Researchers who applied science to management, like the early 20th-century sociologist Frederick Winslow Taylor, often misapplied it by reducing managers to enforcers of ever-smaller tasks. Taylor, in particular, failed to recognize that organizations are people embedded in a culture. Later 20th-century scholars understood the culture-is-us aspect of corporations, but they did not have access to insights from the neuroscience of human sociality because the field only blossomed in the 21st century. Instead, they embraced each psychological fad: Freud, Jung, and Skinner. Or the latest economics and management fads: Six Sigma, Economic Value Added, or the Behavioral Economics of Organizations.[3] In most of these approaches, employees were doled out rewards like so many bread crumbs given to rats. And they hated it.

Managing people as human resources to be exploited for maximum gain produced workplaces that confirmed economists' claims that work provides disutility. Or, in the vernacular: Work is a drag.

Except sometimes it wasn't. There are organizations in which employees love what they do, where they are satisfied professionally and personally by their work, and where they choose to spend their entire careers. This book presents the neuroscience of organizational culture and provides examples of organizations where work is fulfilling and even fun. At these organizations, the disutility of work has mostly disappeared. The practical approach to culture that this book describes is grounded in science and tested in real organizations.

I did not plan to be a culture maven. I run a 25-person neuroscience lab, and I'm trained as an economist and as a neuroscientist. I helped start a field called neuroeconomics that measures brain activity while people make decisions. Neuroeconomics tells us why people do what they do rather than describes their behavior with pejoratives like *irrational*. Perhaps more to the point, I'm the son of an engineer, and my neuroscience experiments are designed to engineer solutions to real problems that real people face.

I've been called a vampire economist because I spend much of my professional life taking blood from willing volunteers to measure neurochemical changes during decisions, just like I was doing in Papua New Guinea. I was the first scientist to show that the brain synthesizes the neurochemical oxytocin when we are trusted and that oxytocin causes us to reciprocate trust by being trustworthy. Oxytocin actually does much more than that, profoundly affecting the way individuals behave socially and the way societies are organized as I reported in my 2012 book *The Moral Molecule*. I spent more than a decade running experiments to document what inhibits and promotes oxytocin release in healthy people, patients with psychiatric and neurologic disorders, and even psychopaths, but my initial research on trust seemed to attract the most attention.

In research I published in 2001, I showed that a culture of trust was among the most powerful predictors economists had ever found to explain why some countries are prosperous while others are poor. High-trust countries have more social interactions that result in more economic transactions that create wealth than do low-trust countries. Trust acts as an economic lubricant, reducing the frictions inherent in economic activity.[4] My research identified the factors that policy makers could affect to increase interpersonal trust and stimulate economic growth.[5] My oxytocin research showed how this occurred in the brain.

After nearly every social science fad failed to produce consistently engaged employees, a number of executives came knocking on my lab's door asking about trust. They believed that interpersonal trust was important for their organizations and thought the science I had done could help them create high-trust cultures. Convinced this was an important problem, I turned my neuroeconomics lens on organizations.

Starting with the mathematics of trusted transactions, I added in what my experiments had shown about the neurochemical signal of trust, oxytocin. From this I surveyed work by neuroscientists and psychologists who were discovering how the brain responds to social interactions. I then put this into a model of culture and compared my model's predictions to what was happening in businesses.[6] I found that high-performance organizations have cultures with high interpersonal trust and highly motivated employees. The cultures in these organizations objectively perform better. The Gallup organization reports that companies with engaged employees are 22 percent more profitable than those in which employees are watching the clock.[7]

Laszlo Bock, senior vice president of People Operations at Google, has written that "culture underpins everything we do at Google."[8] *Culture* was *Merriam-Webster*'s word of the year in 2014. In 2015, the world's largest management consultant, Accenture, identified "optimizing organizational structures for productivity" as a key challenge that organizations face.[9] In other words, culture matters. A lot. While it is fine to talk about culture, a survey of 200,000 employees at over 500 companies reported that 71 percent of companies have mediocre to poor cultures.[10]

My research shows that it is not just any culture but a culture of trust that generates powerful leverage on organizational performance. "Trust between employees and senior management" was the second most important contributor to job satisfaction according to the 2015 Society for Human Resource Management Employee Job Satisfaction and Engagement Survey. Only "respectful treatment of all employees" was chosen more than trust.[11] Google's Project Aristotle studied 180 teams and found that the best predictor of high performance was whether the team had a culture of trust.[12] Fully 50 percent of CEOs think that low trust in their organization is a threat to growth.[13] But most companies have put little effort into closing the trust gap because they are not sure what to do.[14]

In this book, I make a business case that building a culture of trust is essential if an organization is going to be successful. In the book's final chapter, I report multiple streams of data showing that employees in high-trust organizations are substantially more productive, have more energy at work, stay with their employers longer, recommend their workplaces to family and friends, and are significantly more innovative. Those who work in high-trust organizations also more effectively collaborate with coworkers, suffer less chronic stress, and are healthier and happier than employees working at low-trust companies. My research uncovered perhaps the most interesting fact about high-trust organizations: They pay their employees more. The only way this can occur in a competitive labor market is if employees in high-trust companies generate more profit than their low-trust associates.

The business case for creating a high-trust culture also comes from companies that I have worked with, especially those engineering turnarounds. Data from these companies show you how culture reboots have a salubrious effect on employee engagement and multiple business-relevant performance measures. These cases show you how to systematically upgrade your culture so that people work more effectively with each other. I also share data from neuroscience experiments I have run in businesses while employees work that show how trust affects brain activity and employee focus, and motivates a desire to make an extra effort to reach organizational goals. A culture of trust is a powerful lever on human behavior—as long as it is properly implemented.

There is a lot that feels good in this book, and if my findings fit your personal philosophy about work and life, I could not be happier. But unless you have a billion dollars of retained earnings and can do pretty much whatever you want, the data in the book's final chapter prove that creating a human-centric high-trust culture is an absolute necessity to maintain a business's competitive advantage.

Trust profoundly improves organizational performance by providing the foundation for effective teamwork and intrinsic motivation. Trust empowers colleagues to meet objectives in the best way possible while committing them fully to the organization's goals.

Trust requires viewing those with whom one works as whole and complete human beings, not as pieces of human capital. When this occurs, those who work in high-trust organizations not only perform better at work, they are more satisfied with their lives outside of work, being better parents, spouses, and citizens. The effect of trust on quality of life is considerable; Canadian economist John Helliwell and his colleagues found that a 10 percent increase in employee trust in a company's leaders has the same impact on life satisfaction as a 36 percent increase in salary.[15] Creating a culture of trust is exactly where doing good and doing well coincide.

Here's another reason to keep reading. There is a coming war on talent in which hiring and retaining the best employees will be increasingly competitive. Slowing population growth in all developed countries limits workforce entrants, and even today, technically trained individuals are more sought after than ever.[16] The numbers are not pretty. By 2020, labor shortages are projected to be 2.4 million in Germany and over a million each for France, Italy, and the United Kingdom. Because of immigration, the United States will continue to have a labor surplus through 2030, but it already faces shortages of engineers, computer scientists, and data scientists. Even China and Brazil will face labor shortages by 2030.

Business leaders have traditionally assumed that people need to go to work somewhere to earn a salary, so why not here, regardless of the culture? Today, more people are opting for nontraditional ways to earn a living by, for example, creating products on Etsy or reselling items on eBay, renting out rooms in their homes through Airbnb, or driving for Uber or Lyft. People are able to work at home as freelancers on sites like Upwork, Top Coder, or Stack Overflow. LinkedIn has made it much easier to find a traditional job and easier for headhunters to steal talent. The war on talent is fierce and will only become fiercer. Human resources consultants have found that culture is a key way that companies attract and retain the best employees.[17] I show in this book why a culture of trust is an effective way to both engage and retain the best talent. This is especially true for millennials and Gen Xers who want to work for companies they trust and that value their individuality. They are the future of the workforce, and they have substantial bargaining power.[18] Bill George, former chairman and CEO of medical device maker Medtronic, has written, "In business, trust is everything."[19]

Okay, great, so culture matters. How does one create a culture?

In this book, I describe how you can design, monitor, and manage culture for high engagement by creating an environment of trust and accountability. You will learn that trust is an essential part of a high-performance culture because it impacts the triple bottom line: It is good for employees, increases profits, and builds stronger communities.

An organization's performance can be stated as an engineering relationship in which three components determine performance. Those components are denoted by the acronym POP, which stands for people, organization, and purpose. By people I mean selecting the right people for your organization. An enormous number of books have been written about how to hire the right people; I won't rehash them here, though pointers on people selection can be found throughout the book.[20] In short, hiring for a fit to an organization's culture is very important. Tony Hsieh, CEO of the online retailer Zappos.com, has said his company's culture is so important that it does not hire qualified individuals—and has fired employees—who do not live Zappos's culture.[21] Zappos takes the culture fit so seriously that it offers new employees $2,500 to quit after working at Zappos for two weeks if the employee does not think he or she is a good fit, even if those at Zappos do. As you'll read later, my work with Zappos employees bears out the importance of employee fit to culture.

The bulk of this book focuses on organization—that is, designing an organizational culture that is highly engaging for colleagues. Even if you hire the right people, putting them in a dysfunctional or toxic culture inhibits performance. It can even cause your organization to implode—think Enron and WorldCom—but there are many other examples of objectively bad cultures. There are also objectively good cultures, and aspects of company cultures consistent with the neuroscience of high engagement are discussed in detail throughout the book. This provides you with a guide showing what to do and how to do it.

The end of the book discusses the final *P* in the POP relationship: purpose. My neuroscience experiments, and those of many other labs, show that groups of individuals with a clear sense of purpose form strong bonds and perform at high levels. Think of the purpose embodied by members of the U.S. military. Inclusive and engaging cultures generate and sustain commitment to purpose. The studies I have done have revealed the aspects of purpose that matter most as well as how to communicate purpose effectively.

The POP relationship identifies the components leaders can control that cause their organizations to pop with performance. A finding from the science, which was confirmed in my field experiments in businesses, is that trust and purpose synergistically improve organizational performance. It turns out that both trust and purpose activate regions of the brain that motivate cooperation with others, reinforcing behaviors essential to meeting organizational goals. It also means that trust and purpose need to be nurtured by consciously designing living cultures around them.

So why not just run an engagement survey? There are plenty to choose from. Except, their findings are mostly bogus. These surveys ask vague questions about "liking" and "discretionary effort" and often seek to evaluate the rollout of the newest employee engagement program (itself likely based on some psychological fad).

Employees get it. These programs are about making them work harder for no additional benefits. They really come down to "take more, give less." What a bargain! A typical fatal flaw in employee-engagement programs is focusing on "human resources" that can be made to work harder rather than on human beings who may resist this pressure. You have humans at work, not machines.

Another problem with engagement surveys is that they confuse correlation with causation. Many studies, and my own experiments, have shown that people work harder and are happier when things are going well.[22] Better performance improves people's mood and causes them to engage more at work.[23] This book shows how to create a culture in which people voluntarily choose to put in cognitive and emotional effort to further the organization's goals. When colleagues at work enjoy what they do, they go the extra mile, providing amazing customer service, innovating without having to be told to, and staying with the organization for the long term.

Each chapter ends with action items for you to do in your organization. My late colleague at Claremont Graduate University, Peter Drucker, would tell his clients, "Don't tell me what a great meeting you had. Tell me what you are going to do differently Monday morning." In keeping with the engineering approach I'm advocating you take, and in honor of Peter Drucker, I'm calling these end-of-chapter summaries "Monday Morning Lists."

A producer at NHK TV saved my experiment in Malke. He generously flew a staff writer from Tokyo to Cairns, Australia, and then to Papua New Guinea with fresh liquid nitrogen. The film crew even located a working voltage regulator. My equipment was ready.

The villagers in Malke had never been to a doctor or dentist. None had seen their blood flow into a clear tube. You don't live in a rain forest, though, and worry about things that make many Americans nervous. Twenty male volunteers came for their first blood draw. I used this to establish their baseline oxytocin and stress hormone levels.

After these were done, I asked the men to demonstrate their village's culture. They performed an energetic war dance in traditional leaf skirts and animal skins that called on their ancestors for power and bravery. As you will learn in this book, rituals are an effective way to strengthen trust. After 20 minutes, I brought one man after another back to the medical hut for their second blood draw. I centrifuged the tubes and pipetted the plasma into two-milliliter polyethylene microtubes and gently placed them into the freezing canister of liquid nitrogen.

My analysis showed that a majority of the men had released oxytocin during their organization's ritual. Moreover, like the thousands of others I have tested in experiments designed to stimulate oxytocin release, after the ritual, the Malke men said they were more willing to sacrifice to help their community and felt closer to those around them. This is important in a flat organization like Malke.

Chief Edward is not the oldest or the strongest man. He is the most capable. Unlike most of the villagers who may go to the local school for a year or two, Edward completed the fifth grade. He speaks a semblance of English. He regularly commutes to the capital city of the western highlands, Mount Hagen. There he trades locally produced food and woven bags for used clothes, tools, and tobacco. He drives a stubby, four-wheel-drive and is a certified travel guide. There is no doubt that he cares deeply about his village. He is working to create more opportunities for his people through tourism and by promoting education. Some villagers choose to work in the city, but most tire of the hustle and bustle and return to

Malke, where they can grow all the food they need by farming one hour a day. As one villager told me through a translator, "In Malke there is no work." Malkeans choose what they want to do without direction or interference from others.

Chief Edward does not coerce those in Malke to do anything. They are all volunteers in village activities. Villagers who are unable to farm have their plots cared for by relatives or friends so they can eat. No one complains about this. Regular festivals celebrate milestones and successes. Modern businesses, too, depend on people voluntarily choosing to show up, to put their time and creative energy into work, and to lose sleep thinking about a problem they need to solve to help the organization. Yes, they are paid for their efforts, but ultimately all employees are volunteers. They can work elsewhere, or be vagabonds, or go back to school. Money does motivate people, but much less than culture, according to a raft of surveys and the experiments I've run.[24] Peter Drucker wrote, "Management is not culture-free. . . . It is a social function. It is, therefore, both socially accountable and culturally embedded.[25]

As my team loaded the rented four-by-fours for the long drive to Mount Hagen where my blood samples and I would board one of several planes needed to reach my lab, Edward raised his hand and asked me to wait. I had joined his organization and he was my chief, so I waited. The men did another dance to celebrate the experience we had together. Then Edward handed me a package covered in recycled wrapping paper that had been taped together. On it was a card that someone had written in English. It said, "Leaders in our village have hand-spades to tend their plots and feed their people. Since you are a leader, it is important for you to have a hand-spade. Use it wisely for your people." I remember the chief's directive to empower those who work with me every time I see the hand-spade in my lab.

Organizations are universal. So is the release of oxytocin when people interact. Combining these two powerful factors is the secret sauce of high-performance organizations.

☕ MONDAY MORNING LIST

▶ How does your organization treat people as resources rather than humans? Identify one thing you can do to change this.

▶ Investigate if the personalities of your organization's founders are reflected in its present culture. What aspects of this are good and not so good?

▶ The villagers of Malke see each other as members of a unique tribe (there are 800 distinct languages in Papua New Guinea). What makes your organization unique?

▶ Are departments and divisions siloed at your organization? Construct a way to measure if all colleagues know the organization's key objectives.

▶ On a scale from 1 to 7, how trustworthy is your supervisor? Your direct reports? Consider this definition of trustworthiness: A person is trustworthy if he or she completes what is promised and if this cannot be done notifies you so you can make other arrangements.

Chapter 1

The Science of Culture

At Sanganer Camp in north India, the wall dividing the compound from the outside world is two feet high, low enough that even children can climb over it. Sanganer Camp is an open prison village with 170 families and three guards. Each prisoner is serving a life sentence for murder.

Prisoners, all of them men, must be in the camp from 6 p.m. to 6 a.m. but otherwise can work in one of the nearby villages. Their families live with them and are supported by the men's work. In the last decade, there have been only six escapees, and in 50 years, no prisoner has committed another murder. This prison, and others like it in India, grew out of Mahatma Gandhi's view that even prisoners deserve a second chance. Family is important. Most prisoners are entrepreneurs; that is, they start a business to support their families.[1] The mantra at Sanganer is "Trust begets trust."

It turns out that "trust begets trust" is just how the brain works. In experiments I began running in 2001, my lab showed that when someone is tangibly trusted by a stranger, the brain synthesizes the signaling chemical oxytocin. We found that the more trust one is shown, the more the brain produces oxytocin. In these experiments, we measure trust by the amount of money someone takes out of his or her account and transfers to another person—a person who cannot be seen or spoken to but is a real person who is in the experiment. The reason to send money to a stranger is because the experiment is designed so the money grows threefold during the transfer. Here's where it gets really interesting: The amount of oxytocin made by the brain of someone who receives an intentional transfer denoting trust predicts how much money he or she will return to the stranger who had initiated trust—even though the receiver of the largesse is under no obligation to return a penny.

These findings blew a big hole in the traditional view in economics that only a sucker trusts others because trust will never be reciprocated. In fact, 95 percent of the hundreds of people we have tested in experiments who receive money denoting trust release oxytocin. These people show they are trustworthy by returning money to an anonymous person who took a chance to make them better off. This tells us a lot about human nature: Trust begets oxytocin, which begets trustworthiness in return. Think of oxytocin as the biological basis for the Golden Rule: If you treat me nice, my brain makes oxytocin, signaling that you are a person whom I want to be around, so I treat you nice in return. Trust is part of our evolutionarily old repertoire of social behaviors.

How do we know this is true? In these experiments, my lab rapidly drew blood before and after people were trusted in various situations to measure the surge in oxytocin, studies that have been replicated by other labs. But the brain does many things simultaneously. So to prove causation, we developed a way to safely infuse synthetic oxytocin into living human brains (through the nose). In these experiments, those receiving oxytocin, compared to those who got a placebo, showed more trust in strangers by sending them more money, and the use of oxytocin more than doubled the number of people who sent *all* of their money to a stranger, exhibiting maximal trust.

The full story of this discovery and how oxytocin provides new insights into human nature and human society is not essential to understand how trust makes companies perform. The most important thing to know is that oxytocin works by activating a brain network that makes us more empathic. For gregariously social creatures like human beings, empathy is a valuable skill. Almost everyone over six years old can cognitively forecast what someone is likely to do by putting himself or herself in the other's shoes (this is called having a theory of mind). This ability helps us understand how others will behave. But empathy gives us additional information about others; it tells us how another person is feeling, or is likely to feel, in various situations. This tells us *why* someone is doing something.

I call oxytocin the moral molecule because when the brain releases it, we treat others well, like we would a family member. Oxytocin-stimulated empathy means if we were to hurt someone, we would share that person's pain. Since we do not like pain, empathy motivates appropriate social/moral behaviors. Human beings have highly developed empathy because it makes us more effective social beings. Prosocial behaviors like being trustworthy sustain us in communities of other people, including in organizations. As social creatures, we only survive in groups, so having the neurologic capacity for empathy and thereby an enhanced understanding of appropriate social behaviors has increased our likelihood of survival. But it gets even better than that: Oxytocin makes it feel good to be part of an organization. Our brains reward us for cooperating and treating others well, including being trustworthy when we are trusted. Trust begets trust.

The neuroscience gets really interesting when we go beyond what human brains do on average (scientists' favorite phrase) and ask where the variations in human behaviors come from. A large part of my research on oxytocin over the last decade (using several million dollars of research money) went into determining what promotes or inhibits oxytocin release. Isn't that the key question? Why does your colleague who gets promoted turn into a raging jerk? Or, why do you soften your "it's all about the numbers" stance when reprimanding a colleague when you learn his young daughter is ill? Our social brain changes its activity to help us adapt to the people around us and to our own physiologic state. That means that even though I am sure you are a good person, I know that sometimes you yell at your spouse or are snarky with a clerk when shopping. From your brain's perspective, treating the people around you with kindness is usually, but not always, the right response.

Here's the science. High levels of stress inhibit the release of oxytocin. You know this already: When you are stressed out you are not your best self. Most everyone understands this short-term failing and will accept an apology for a transgression. By the time we are six or seven years old, we recognize social transgressions. Everyone around us is giving us feedback, subtly and not so subtly, on whether our behavior is appropriate or not. Constantly. Oxytocin and the brain circuit it activates function as a moral compass, telling us what our social group believes is right or wrong. Each group establishes a culture, a set of social norms that we transmit to group members explicitly, often through stories, and implicitly when we provide feedback to others through facial expressions and by our actions.

The other potent oxytocin inhibitor is a chemical that has a profound effect on brain activity: testosterone. My group has shown in experiments in which we dosed men with synthetic testosterone that it causes them to be selfish and entitled; that is, high-testosterone males share less with others and demand more from others.[2] It's all about them. You already know who the least empathic humans on the planet are: young males. Men have five to ten times more testosterone than women (and get in more fights, take more risks, and commit more crimes), and competition and status increase testosterone in both sexes. Promotion? Testosterone goes up. Hot new romantic partner? Ditto. Earned a $2 million bonus this year? You might just become an unmitigated ass if you are not thoughtful about putting a check on your behavior. Testosterone whispers to our brains that we have won the social lottery and makes us behave like demigods. It also increases libido. No surprise that CEOs, presidents, and movie stars have affairs.

But nature modulates aggressive behaviors. After age 30, testosterone begins to fall in men and continues thereafter. The good news is that a man's ability to behave prosocially generally increases with age. You can actively promote oxytocin release and capture its benefits, including increased interpersonal trust and improved health, by modifying your default social behaviors. I'm a six-foot-four high-testosterone former jock, but I earned the nickname "Dr. Love" by actively forging connections with everyone I meet. One way I do this is by hugging people when I first meet them. My lab has shown that touch causes the brain to make oxytocin. A hug is a "brain hack" that stimulates an immediate, though temporary, emotional attachment. If I can do it, you can, too. As we'll discover in the chapters that follow, the goal is to seek a balance between the high motivation and drive we get from testosterone and the cooperation and teamwork that come from releasing oxytocin.

Let me illustrate the amazing neural ballet the brain does at work by describing an experiment I ran on a rugby team.[3] Rugby, like business, requires intraorganization cooperation and interorganization competition. By taking blood before and after ruggers warmed up for a match, I found that the warm-up caused increases in oxytocin, testosterone, and fast-acting stress hormones. Most interestingly, oxytocin levels went from being dissimilar before the warm-up to being more similar afterward. The rugby players were clearly pumped up for the match as evidenced by the increase in testosterone and stress hormones, but their brains discriminated between teammates and competitors in order to cooperate to win the match. This is exactly what an effective culture does at work: It focuses colleagues on cooperation to overcome the competition. Oxytocin and the neurochemicals with which it interacts can be harnessed to maximize teamwork at work.

Every biological system, including the brain, is an economic system. The brain has limited resources that it seeks to deploy efficiently in order to help us survive and thrive. The brain doesn't burn the calories to synthesize oxytocin without a stimulus for its production. (Actually, a little bit of oxytocin is made all the time just to keep the system working, but this does not affect social behaviors.) While a smile at colleagues or an "attaboy" out of the blue can induce a small oxytocin spike and the attendant increase in cooperation, moderate stress endured as a group is an effective oxytocin stimulant. When your team is working on a big project, you have to come together and get things done. The memory of petty slights and personality quirks fades as teamwork takes over. Oxytocin has been shown to increase not only trust and cooperation but also forgiveness. So it is easier to apologize for past failings when working together intensively (just in case you want to resolve those issues).

I have tested oxytocin release in the bedroom, board room, and bivouac. It occurs everywhere. I have documented more than a dozen ways to stimulate oxytocin production in my experiments. All it takes is a positive social interaction without too much stress or testosterone. Oxytocin just might be the molecule that makes us human. At least it is the molecule that creates our humanity.[4] By understanding a little about the neuroscience of oxytocin, you can harness humanity at work. Believe me, the people at work want this.

A key takeaway from this chapter is that culture is not static. It evolves as the people and purpose of the organization change. Most importantly, culture can be managed and continuously improved to increase engagement by volunteer-employees. Next, we'll learn how the neuroscience I've done can be applied to improve your organization's culture.

A culture in which oxytocin is released through positive social interactions is one way to keep people engaged at work, but there are other ways. Many organizations use a fear-based management approach. This has been called Theory X.[5] The science shows that fear-based management is a losing proposition because people acclimate to fear quickly. Fear-inducing leaders must ramp up threats to increase productivity, but there are only so many threats one can make.

There are significant downsides to using fear-based management that treats people like replaceable capital and ignores the role of culture. The most prominent is high turnover as colleagues flee dysfunctional companies. The cost of replacing colleagues is high, from 20 to 200 percent of their annual salary, so creating an engaging culture at work also motivates people to keep showing up.[6]

The stepson of Theory X management is the use of money to motivate colleagues. This idea was popularized by the "scientific management" approach of Frederick Winslow Taylor. Taylor advocated breaking down work into small tasks and rewarding each completed task.[7] Yet survey after survey shows that money is a weak motivator of performance; a recent meta-analysis confirmed this.[8] If you are counting on the golden cage (high pay) to motivate people, you will lose. This approach creates indentured servants rather than enthusiastic volunteers. Since everyone cannot be paid above average, it means junior associates are typically underpaid and often overworked, trying their best to get into the golden cage, but they often endure disengagement and burnout once they get there.

People are paid for their work, but creating the opportunity to express one's intrinsic motivation is the best way to achieve high performance over the long haul.[9] Think of creating an organizational culture where people would choose to come to work even if they were not being paid. That is an organization that thrives on intrinsic motivation. A test of this is the 3 a.m. rule. Highly intrinsically motivated employees send the occasional email in the middle of the night because they are obsessed with solving some problem. If leaders never get 3 a.m. emails, then either intrinsic motivation is low or the objectives of the organization are not challenging enough to motivate outside-of-work rumination.

A simple way to move away from extrinsic incentives to intrinsic motivation is to banish the terms *employee, human resource,* or even *talent* to describe those with whom one works. People who choose to come to work and expend effort to help an organization achieve its goals need to be seen as fully developed human beings. Everyone at work is a person with goals and hopes, emotions and a personal life, skills and options. I prefer to call those with whom I work "colleagues," and I'll use this language throughout the book. I also advocate changing the name of human resources departments to human development departments. This change signals that the organization is committed to engaging colleagues with challenges at work while maintaining an appropriate work-life integration.

The culture-to-performance model upon which this book is based is presented in Figure 1. The neuromanagement challenge is to design a culture in which oxytocin can be released many times during the day by positive social interactions. Understanding the

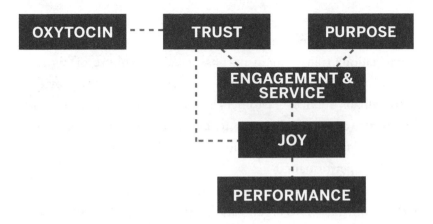

FIGURE 1. How oxytocin creates trust and improves mood
and organizational performance.

brain circuit that oxytocin activates has allowed me to identify a set of actionable ways to design organizational cultures that bolster and sustain interpersonal trust. The empirical tests of this model confirm its efficacy for building trust and for inspiring performance.

To make it easier to remember the classes of management policies that build trust, I've devised a catchy mnemonic. The eight factors that the neuroscience affirms are the building blocks of organizational trust have the acronym OXYTOCIN. This stands for Ovation, eXpectation, Yield, Transfer, Openness, Caring, Invest, and Natural. More than just identifying these factors, the science done by my lab and others provides precise prescriptions for the implementation of the OXYTOCIN policies for maximal impact on brain and behavior. My empirical tests of the model in for-profit and nonprofit organizations show that together the OXYTOCIN factors explain 100 percent of the variation in organizational trust. Thus, there are no other classes of management policies that influence trust.

The model shows that the OXYTOCIN factors can be used as leverage to increase organizational trust. Trust, combined with an organization's transcendent purpose, creates a culture of high engagement. Enthusiastic colleagues delight customers by providing extraordinary service. Customers are appreciative and express their happiness, causing colleagues to experience joy at work ("Joy"). When colleagues get this positive feedback, the organization sustains high performance.

In the chapters that follow, I define each factor, report its individual contribution to organizational trust (the coefficient of variation known as R^2 in statistics), and provide examples of organizations that have implemented culture interventions to improve performance. Each of the OXYTOCIN factors explains between 51 percent and 84 percent of the variation in organizational trust. These data come from a nationally representative sample in the United States of working people who have taken the Ofactor survey that I developed. The OXYTOCIN factors are not statistically independent (each factor shares some of the contribution to organizational trust with other factors), so that the sum of the individual coefficients of variation exceeds 1.

In just a moment, I will ask you to take the Ofactor survey to measure trust and the OXYTOCIN factors in your organization. The survey has only 30 questions, so the time commitment is low. By taking the survey before you read the remaining chapters, you can focus on the OXYTOCIN factors that are lowest in your organization—these are the first places you will want to intervene to improve teamwork and performance.

None of the management policies that influence trust are new; managers since the Industrial Revolution have tried everything under the sun to affect performance. What is new is that neuroscience provides a framework to understand how culture impacts intrinsic motivation so that policy changes are not made willy-nilly. Equally importantly, the neuroscience shows how to optimize the impact of management policies that affect trust to accelerate performance.

I would like you to think of management as a series of small-scale controlled experiments. In this chapter, I lay out a methodology that you can use to improve your culture in a systematic way through changes in management policies. Peter Drucker wrote, "Your first and foremost job as a leader is to take charge of your own energy and then help to orchestrate the energy of those around you." Yet most leaders are so whipsawed by the hurly-burly of work that they have few resources left to energize their teams. You can do this more effectively by tweaking your organizational culture to permit your colleagues to put more energy into their projects. An improved culture also gives leaders more time to focus their energy on what they do best. You do not need to go from 30 miles per hour to 100 in a single day. Rather, you should slowly and steadily step on the accelerator so that you safely reach 100 miles an hour without the wheels falling off.

The first step in any experiment is measurement. The more improvements you want to make in your culture, the more you have to measure it. Knowing your baseline is important, but so is knowing about cyclic variations in culture. Are people disengaged on Mondays? Are they stressed at the end of a quarter because of deadlines? Does telecommuting diminish or accentuate trust? Every organization will have different answers to these questions, and you cannot know how to improve culture until you first measure it.

The second step in an experiment is to identify an intervention you want to test. *Test* is the key word here. Leaders are not gods, omniscient in the methods that can be used to improve performance. Neither am I. Once you have a framework to understand how to create an engaging culture, you must choose the interventions you want to test. Management experiments rigorously test interventions to ensure they actually work. The try-and-test method is a humble approach to management. Listen to those around you, communicate clearly what you seek to do, and then roll out the change. This book explains why this humble approach engages your employees much more than the traditional top-down, "Do it because I say so" approach.

An intervention in medicine might be testing a new drug on sick patients. In management, your intervention is a policy change. For example, this book explains why having a vacation policy is a bad idea. A management policy change would involve explaining to colleagues—in person if possible—why your organization is getting rid of a fixed number of vacation days and is instead allowing people to choose how they manage their time themselves.

The third step in an experiment is to determine the outcome(s) you seek to influence. Is it sales? Health care expenditures? Profits? Employee turnover? Perhaps it is several of these. Concreteness is the key. To assess impact, measure outcomes before the policy change, and then choose a reasonable period for changes to take effect. You then measure again. If the policy change improved performance measures, stick with it. If it did not affect outcomes, you can always return to the status quo. In either case, pick the next intervention you want to test and repeat the cycle. You need to continuously manage culture because if you do not, it evolves on its own as the people in the organization and the mission change.

Management experiments are related to the PDCA (Plan Do Check Act) Deming cycle, which itself is based on the scientific method as described by Francis Bacon (1561–1626). It is also similar to Six Sigma's DMAIC (Define, Measure, Analyze, Improve, Control). What you are already doing to optimize your production process or supply chain is what you will now do for culture.

Peter Drucker said, "Successful application always demands adaptation, cutting, fitting, trying, balancing. It always demands testing against reality before there is final commitment." If the management intervention did not improve a performance metric, you can always try something different. After all, it was just an experiment. As long as you communicate this clearly to colleagues, they will get on board because all the interventions are human centric: They are designed to improve the lives of your colleagues as well as organizational performance.

To summarize, here's the way to run a management experiment:

▸ Obtain baseline data for the policy you want to change and key outcome variables you believe it affects.

▸ Communicate to colleagues the reason for the change, the date the change will occur, and the period of the test.

▸ At the end of the test period, confirm that the policy you sought to change actually did change, and measure outcome variables.

▸ If the change had a positive effect on outcome measures, continue with it. If not, consider returning to the status quo.

▸ Lather, rinse, and repeat.

Think of this book as an engineering guide to getting the "soft stuff" right. The next eight chapters show you how to implement policy interventions to improve business-relevant outcomes. I do this by describing the science and then providing examples from businesses that have happened across trust-enhancing policies. These are guides for you to follow in your organization.

The subversive motif of this book is that there is no optimal organizational culture. Unlike in the hypothetical world that economic theorists enjoy inhabiting, your culture depends on the founder's personality, industry norms, the executives in charge, and a host of other constraining factors. The optimum is never achievable. Your goal should be to continuously make improvements in the culture. And don't get stuck in analysis paralysis, seeking perfection; it is better to be approximately right than exactly wrong.

Management is a humanity, literally. But it is also one that can be understood through the lens of science. I believe that management that blends humanity and (neuro)science is the most effective. It is a process, not an end point. Laszlo Bock, head of PeopleOps at Google, has said, "Building a great culture and environment requires constant learning, experimentation, and renewal. But, it's worth it."[10]

☕ MONDAY MORNING LIST

▸ Take the Ofactor survey at Ofactor.com/book to measure trust in your organization and the eight factors that create trust. You will also get data on Purpose and Joy.

▸ Write down three to five performance measures that you think your culture affects. Determine how to measure these objectively.

▸ Identify a division or department that runs effectively. Write down three reasons that you think this microculture performs so well.

▸ Ask colleagues to name one thing they would change in your organization. How might trust affect the things people want to change?

▸ Talk to colleagues to see how they would raise trust at work.

Chapter 2

Ovation

Ovation recognizes colleagues who contribute to the organization's success. Ovation explains 67 percent of organizational trust.

The Container Store does Ovation in brass. And straw. And chocolate. Ovation has always been part of its culture, but it was difficult to sustain in the Great Recession. Canceling the annual staff meeting at its Dallas headquarters was one of the cuts it had to make. A typical staff meeting brought 300 to 350 senior associates from retail stores nationwide to discuss the next year's strategies, products, and programs.

When rosier financials permitted the reboot of the staff meeting in 2011, the theme was "Connection, Communication, and Community." It included a roster of inspirational speakers, including Roy Spence, founder of GSD&M advertising agency; John Mackey, founder of Whole Foods; and Bert Jacobs, who, with his brother John, founded clothing store Life is Good. The Container Store founder Kip Tindell invited me to speak as well. The three *C*'s in its 2011 theme are right in my wheelhouse, and I spoke for an hour about organizations as communities and the science of connection. All the talks were recorded and were later made available for viewing by associates who did not attend the meeting.

When I walked into The Container Store's headquarters, I happened to meet its first employee, a woman who still worked there 32 years later. In fact, President Melissa Reiff told me that turnover at The Container Store is very low, averaging about 10 percent annually in its retail stores, compared to an industry average of 27 percent for part-time colleagues.[1] Ovation is a key reason for this.

The first thing one sees at The Container Store's headquarters is the wall of fame, a set of glass plaques listing every employee who has worked at The Container Store 10 years or more. Associates earn new plaques for every half decade of additional service. Every time a new plaque is earned, the associate and his or her spouse are flown to Dallas and feted by the senior executives, including a weekend at the Four Seasons and fancy meals. This Ovation recognizes their service to the company and customers.

I could feel the Ovation when I walked into their headquarters. Because it releases oxytocin, I hugged everyone I met rather than shook hands. Everyone was pleased to hug me, from associates to C-suite executives. There was palpable care shown by colleagues toward each other. The entire meeting was joyous and celebratory; the company had survived the recession and was poised to grow again.

An Ovation that I helped The Container Store strengthen is called "We Love Our Employees Day." On Valentine's Day, every employee receives a gift basket that includes a "love note" from the founders, T-shirts, chocolates, and other fun gifts. In 2010, the company put a 50,000 square foot "love note" to its employees on the roof of its headquarters. Flying into Dallas recently, I saw that the love note was still on the roof. The company has also purchased full-page ads stating, "We Love Our Employees!" in the *New York Times* and the *Dallas Morning News*. As love songs play in stores, customers are encouraged to go to the company's website and leave "love notes" to show appreciation for their favorite employees.

I discovered that The Container Store not only celebrates its employees, it does the same for customers. I received a gift certificate as part of my compensation for speaking and several months later drove an hour to the Pasadena, California, store with my daughter to use it. Within five minutes, associates who had been in Dallas or had seen the video of my presentation introduced themselves with hugs. They took me around the store as if I were a celebrity. And yes, I made a raft of purchases.

Most amazingly, a year after my talk in Dallas, I received an email from Melissa Reiff. It said in part,

> A week doesn't pass that I don't hear from many employees who reference your presentation, or something you said to them in a one-on-one conversation that continues to have a lasting impact on their thinking and behavior. They are leading in a more conscious way, they are more aware of their wake, they are more involved in their local communities, they have connected with their colleagues and our customers in even more authentic ways, and they have strengthened their personal relationships. You wouldn't believe the hundreds of responses that I received and specifically how YOUR presentation made a difference. Here is just a handful that I wanted to share with you.

Her email included half a dozen laudatory comments that were made about my presentation by associates. I was blown away by her kindness. She runs a company with 6,000 employees and nearly a billion dollars in revenue. I had been paid for my speech at the staff meeting, and that could have ended our relationship—she did not have to spend the time to thank me a year later. I realized that The Container Store thrives on Ovation, it was part of the company's culture, and it instinctively created Ovation everywhere.

A recent Maritz survey reports that only 10 percent of employees are completely satisfied with their company's recognition programs.[2] And yet, 55 percent of those surveyed agreed that Ovation improves their job performance. This is an enormous disconnect. A global survey of 100,000 employees reported that 79 percent said that a "lack of appreciation" was a primary reason they quit their jobs.[3] Organizations that have at least one recognition program have a lower turnover rate than no-Ovation businesses. By one estimate, a 5 percent increase in colleague retention increases profitability by 25 to 85 percent.[4] As Dean Kamen, legendary inventor of the Segway and many other ingenious products, told me at an innovation conference at Google, "You get what you celebrate."[5]

The last chapter directed you to take the Ofactor survey so you know how well your organization does Ovation. Now I'm going to help you improve your Ovation.

Unexpected, tangible, and personal. Neuroscience provides specific and actionable ways you can maximize the impact of Ovation. There are two routes through which Ovation affects the brain and thereby motivation and teamwork. First, Ovation can cause the direct release of the neurotransmitter dopamine in the brain. This occurs when one anticipates a reward. Dopamine increases focus and energy and provides a feel-good mood boost. If you've ever played poker, even for low stakes, you know this feeling. You really want to win the pot, and as a result, your brain becomes laser focused on calculating odds, devising strategies, and seeking to read the other players' "tells." And if you do win, you feel fabulous. Ovation uses the same neurologic mechanism to engage colleagues at work.

Dopamine's effect is most powerful when Ovation is unexpected, tangible, and personal. Ovation links recognition with the goal that was met and reinforces the intrinsic reward of helping the team achieve success. The personal part is important. If a team member receiving Ovation is a chocolate lover, purchase a fancy box of chocolates as a gift. Then, present the Ovation at your next all-hands meeting, or the day the project finishes. When the reward is tangible, seeing it after the initial Ovation and showing it to colleagues or one's spouse strengthens the neural pathways linking achievement to reward.

The other dopamine driver is making the reward unexpected. The brain loves surprises because it means something new has happened, and this focuses our attention on it. By the way, unexpected does not mean that Ovation cannot be scheduled. It just means that the person or team receiving an Ovation should not know it is coming or what it is.

Close in time and consistent. Another way to harness the reinforcing effects of dopamine is to engage in Ovation close in time to the goal being met or exceeded. Ovation weeks or months later can be boring and does not strongly reinforce the link between "We did it!" and "We were recognized for it!" in the brain. Ovation needs to occur consistently and promptly. Dopamine is part of the brain's arousal system, so you can produce stronger activation in the brain by creating Ovations that are exciting. Take your team tandem skydiving after finishing the big project? Yes! Tickets to Disney World? Go for it!

A good rule of thumb is that Ovation should occur no longer than one week after meeting a challenge. And move Ovation around. If every goal that is met produces an Ovation, its power is diminished. When big goals are met, Ovation must be done. For smaller goals, a simple thank-you at an all-hands meeting is often enough. Ovation for small things is very important; it should become a constant practice in your organization. Volunteer-employees always need to be thanked.

Public Ovation. Ovation can stimulate oxytocin release when recognition is done in public. Ovation that is public, and especially when it comes from peers or customers, builds attachment to team members and makes one's job more enjoyable. Public Ovation can even include family or friends to more strongly reinforce how much those in the organization value meeting goals. It turns out that oxytocin synthesis also induces the brain to make dopamine. By creating Ovation that is unexpected and public, you can harness the double whammy of oxytocin and dopamine co-release in the brain.

Public peer recognition is an effective way to stimulate Ovation regularly. Consider setting up a system to allow peers to recognize each other by, for example, awarding points colleagues can use to get gifts or trips. Zappos.com uses Zappos dollars, or Zollars, to thank peers for answering questions or volunteering to help. Zollars can be redeemed for gifts, given to another peer, or donated to charity at their dollar value. Importantly, Zollars include a note from the person doing the Ovation stating why it came from that individual, further personalizing its impact. Peer Ovation encourages everyone to celebrate accomplishments.

Discovering best practices. I first tested many of the ideas developed here in the 25-person neuroscience laboratory I direct. I initiate Ovation at our Monday all-hands meeting by asking the team to offer verbal gratitudes for extraordinary performance by their colleagues. I usually offer one or two myself. I follow this with a gift given publicly. Sometimes this is a $25 coffee card for a peer Ovation or a more personal gift if I'm offering an Ovation to a colleague myself. When the gift is offered, inevitably the person being recognized tells the group how others helped him or her meet the goal or solve the problem that produced the Ovation.

This aspect of Ovation is very important: Ovation provides a forum to discuss best practices. It does this from a peer perspective rather than as a dictate from the top floor. These peer-based discussions are often absorbed and remembered better than mandated training because they are told in the form of a personal story (more on this in chapter 10). Ovation provides a natural setting to share information between colleagues. In addition, public Ovation generates aspirations in colleagues who are not being recognized to achieve Ovation for themselves and their teams, activating the dopamine motivation system in the brain, further improving performance.

Ovation reinforces the importance of teamwork and uses group goals to motivate colleagues. Research by psychologist Carol Dweck and her collaborators has shown that Ovation only improves performance when the person is recognized for completing a task, not just for showing up. The "You are great" type of Ovation is, Dweck finds, stressful and disincentivizing. We cannot be perfect all the time (more on this in chapter 9), so we should not set up this unattainable goal. Praising the task someone has done has a positive impact on future motivation and performance. It also identifies what is valued by those in the organization.

It should now be clear why the "Employee of the Month" parking space has little impact on engagement and performance. Most employees realize that this perk is moved around the entire unit on a monthly basis until nearly everyone has "earned" it. The predictability, lack of linkage to a goal being met, and impersonal nature substantially diminish the impact on colleague motivation. This is the value of using neuroscience to guide management policies: By understanding how Ovation affects the brain, the science identifies how to achieve the maximal impact on performance.

Public and private. A corollary to public Ovation is that you should praise in public but critique in private. Public dressing-down of colleagues causes a spike in stress hormones. This makes your targets defensive and aggressive, inhibiting oxytocin release and therefore trust. Those who witness this aggression can't help but think "I could be next," further eroding trust. When trust is low, engagement and performance suffer. Social stressors rev up our physiology 50 percent longer than nonsocial stressors. In fact, social condemnation activates the same pathways in the brain that process physical pain. Being humiliated at work triggers brain activity that is just like getting punched in the gut.[6]

Remember to treat colleagues as volunteers. If a colleague is missing a goal, work with him or her privately. You might move this associate to another project, or offer additional training, rather than yelling, "You never get your work done!" Leadership is about developing the human potential around you. It is not an opportunity to threaten or intimidate others.

A key difference in the Ofactor management approach, compared to traditional management practice inherited from the 19th century, is the lack of threats and fear. Fear is a fine short-term motivator but a poor long-term one. Worse than having no effect, when leaders spew out threats at work, it engenders learned helplessness in which people just give up trying to do anything. A rat that is randomly shocked in its cage quite quickly just sits still and takes the shocks rather than tries to avoid the unavoidable. The rat eventually stops moving and dies. Learned helplessness is the opposite of motivation. Fear-based management undermines employee trust, engagement, health, and retention (you'll see the data on this in chapter 11).

Even the sluggish U.S. government has accepted the need for Ovation to sustain performance and retain highly skilled colleagues. The 1993 Government Performance and Results Act (amended and extended in 2010) permits government agencies to use monetary and nonmonetary Ovation to recognize outstanding performance by civil servants. Most incentives are worth less than $750, and some agencies overuse Ovation programs, with nearly all colleagues receiving recognition. But, if the U.S. government has realized the importance of Ovation, for-profits and nonprofits should, too.

Ovation significantly impacts retention even in high-turnover industries. CarMax, the largest used-car retailer in the United States, uses Ovation to keep its best salespeople. The average annual employee turnover rate in the car sales industry is 50 percent. At CarMax, only 17 percent of colleagues leave the company in an average year. In fact, CarMax is consistently included in *Fortune* magazine's Best Companies to Work For list. CEO Tom Folliard understands that Ovation is not about money. Colleagues are recognized for performing great service to customers through more than a dozen national programs and many more local ones. A monthly email called "Tom's Top Ten" recognizes top-performing stores with winners receiving a "big sandwich" party. One of the most beloved programs by associates is CarMax's steak cookouts, events for high-performing stores where executives do the grilling and serve the food to everyone else. People are lining up to work for CarMax—it receives nearly a quarter million applications annually.

A classic study of American and British managerial trainees who received Ovation after performing several tasks showed substantial increases in performance compared to those who were not recognized. Ovation directed to Americans produced an average 103 percent increase in performance while the British had a 45 percent jump. Yet a 2011 study by the Maritz Institute revealed that only 46 percent of sales personnel receive any Ovation at all. Two-thirds of employees say Ovation makes them happy to be at work.[7] Omitting Ovation is an enormous missed opportunity.

Love or money. A Boston Consulting Group survey found that Ovation is the most important thing colleagues want at work. Salary? That was number eight on the list.[8] One's salary provides extrinsic motivation, but study after study has shown that one's internal drive, or intrinsic motivation, is the key to sustaining performance in the long term. Add to this the motivation of being part of a trusted team, and social motivation is added to the mix. As we'll see in chapter 9, social motivation is most powerful when an organization's purpose is clearly defined and is communicated internally and externally.

Effective Ovation generally avoids giving people money. A study at a large Dutch company tested a variety of incentives to motivate employees to reduce energy consumption. Monetary rewards for reducing energy use—given in public and private—had little effect on behavior, producing energy savings between 1 and 3 percent. But public acknowledgment of savings had a powerful effect on energy use, reducing average usage by 6.4 percent. That is, social motivation improved performance by up to 500 percent over monetary incentives. Importantly, the energy savings persisted for eight weeks after the recognition program ended.

Cash rewards must be used with care because they can significantly degrade performance. Studies of incentive programs such as bonus payments show that they can inhibit performance by destroying intrinsic motivation. That is, extrinsic motivation crowds out intrinsic motivation. Explicit pay-to-play programs can cause colleagues to feel as though their actions are being controlled externally. As we'll discuss in chapter 5, when colleagues have control over how, when, and where they do their work, performance is enhanced. A large number of laboratory and field experiments have shown that monetary rewards decrease productivity. Working in a solely extrinsically motivated organization can also undermine physical and mental health.[9]

Recognizing peers. Professor Michael Norton of Harvard Business School and his colleagues conducted a study at a Belgian pharmaceutical company in which salespeople were given one of two types of monetary incentives. In the "personal" condition, participants were given 15 euros and were instructed to spend it on themselves. In the "social" condition, the instructions asked salespeople to give the 15 euros to peers on their sales team. Norton's team then tracked sales for the following month.

The results were telling. The personal incentive increased average sales by only 4.5 euros. In contrast, the social incentive increased sales by 78 euros. Giving a gift to a peer produced a 500 percent return on investment.

To confirm its results, Norton's team used the same incentive scheme for a group of intermural college dodgeball teams. Before the incentive intervention, teams had a 50 percent chance of winning each game they played during a season. Norton then introduced the individual or social incentive system to the teams. The personal bonus had no effect on winning (in fact, the winning percentage declined slightly to 43 percent). But using the bonus to benefit team members increased the average winning percentage from 50 percent to 81 percent. This confirms the results of the Belgian study: Social Ovation is powerful.

Friends and family. The oxytocin-dopamine Ovation double whammy can be achieved when friends and family are included in celebrations. Starbucks in China, which has around 1,200 stores and 20,000 employees, recently began including families in its Ovations. Starbucks CEO Howard Schultz said he had this idea because China's one-child law produces extraordinarily tight-knit families. After attending a recent family-included Ovation, Schultz watched parents become highly emotional when their adult children received recognition for their work; the employees, in turn, mirrored their parents' outpouring of emotions. Schultz realized that working at Starbucks was not only important for employees but for their families, and that this needed to be recognized and celebrated.

The American manufacturing conglomerate Barry-Wehmiller Companies includes family in Ovation but puts it on steroids. Barry-Wehmiller owns and operates around 60 small manufacturers of production automation equipment in North America and Europe. Most of the businesses owned by Barry-Wehmiller were acquired and reorganized to be profitable, retaining the companies' original names and most of the original staff.

Barry-Wehmiller CEO Robert "Bob" Chapman told me that he loves to do Ovation big. Bob is a sports-car enthusiast and said he thought many of the people working in the various businesses he runs would also enjoy driving a sports car. "Why can't business be fun?" he asked. "Why do we go to work to make a living, and go home and use our money to have fun?"[10]

So Bob bought several bright yellow Chevy SSRs. Then he and his team started a program in which employees at each company could nominate a peer who made a "positive impact on their life." The language here is important: This recognition is not for someone who did an excellent job or helped others succeed at work; it is designed to be more broadly focused. The submissions are used to identify an exemplary colleague. Here's where Barry-Wehmiller's Ovation gets interesting (and neurological). The winner is kept secret, and each plant is closed on the day of the Ovation. The chosen employee's family and close friends are invited to attend the ceremony (without tipping off the winner). The entire company comes out for the celebration, and the nominating letters about the winner are read to the assemblage. The Ovation concludes with the recipient getting the keys to the yellow Chevy to drive for a week. Bob told me that nearly every recipient goes first to his or her parent's house and takes Mom for a ride.[11]

Being recognized for one's above-and-beyond performance is very important for social creatures like human beings. The impact of Ovation is compounded by including colleagues, family, and friends. Ovations done big also spread the desire widely among others to have one's own Ovation. Bob Chapman has written, "People are the most important asset we have. . . . What we have found in business through these simple gestures is that people have a craving, a tremendous need, to feel appreciated."[12] Barry-Wehmiller's key focus is not on manufacturing or profits but on "building great people." Many other well-run companies, including IKEA and Pella, use peer Ovation to recognize excellence. But few of them go as big as Barry-Wehmiller.

Bob Chapman's view, consistent with the data in chapter 11, is that organizations are embedded in cultures, and cultures that celebrate their members perform better.

☕ MONDAY MORNING LIST

▸ Start an Ovation program or modify an existing one to recognize top performers weekly.

▸ Create a fun annual public Ovation for the top individual or division.

▸ Use Ovation to identify and document best practices; adopt these practices in other divisions.

▸ Create a peer Ovation program that recognizes exemplary colleagues.

▸ Write down a set of personal gifts for those on your team that would be appropriate for future Ovations.

Chapter 3

eXpectation

eXpectation occurs when colleagues face a challenge as a group. eXpectation explains 83 percent of organizational trust.

Work colleagues hate surprises (unless they are Ovations). But two out of three employees are surprised by the feedback in their annual performance reviews. Compare that to how often supervisors check in with highly engaged employees: weekly.[1] Those who get weekly feedback are rarely surprised.

From the perspective of the brain, anything that happened more than a few weeks ago is nearly irrelevant, so waiting a year to give employees feedback on their performance is simply useless. Regular feedback on performance builds neural pathways in the brain that adapt behavior to meet goals. I call this eXpectation.

It's actually better than that: Setting difficult but achievable eXpectations engages the brain's reward system so that meeting goals at work becomes highly engaging and enjoyable. This chapter shows you how to establish eXpectations for your colleagues by designing challenges.

Several years ago, I agreed to appear on the TV show *Through the Wormhole with Morgan Freeman*. The producers asked me to create an exciting experiment to illustrate why we trust strangers—sometimes with our lives. I thought that tandem skydiving was the perfect thing to test. The kicker was, I would be the test subject.

Like most people, I have an appropriate fear of heights. Okay, perhaps more than appropriate, but I function fine most of the time. Skydiving was not something I ever really wanted to do. In the weeks prior to my skydive, I suffered panic attacks and terrible dreams that left me sweating. Once the appointed day arrived and the cameras were rolling, there was no place to go but up. An hour before the plane lifted off a dirt track at Skydive Perris in Perris, California, I took a sample of my blood to get a baseline for oxytocin and stress hormones. I planned to jab my arm with a needle immediately after I reached the ground and take more blood. How would my brain respond to free fall?

With only 10 minutes of instruction, I was strapped to a skydive instructor named Andy. I watched the altimeter on my wrist as the hollowed-out 1960s prop plane circled higher. At 12,500 feet, a green light came on and the jumpmaster opened a side door. As the wind rushed in, the instructor and I waddled toward the abyss. A graduate student who had come along gave me a set of cognitive tests before I stepped out. I failed half of them. I was extraordinarily focused on what I had to do to get into free-fall position safely. With a "1, 2, 3, go," we plunged 7,500 feet in 50 seconds. The parachute opened at 5,000 feet, and we drifted down like babies tethered to a nylon bassinet.

What did my brain do? Not surprisingly, my stress hormones went up over 400 percent. Testosterone—responding to the extreme challenge—went up 40 percent. The surprise was that my oxytocin rose by 17 percent. I'll confess I felt a strong attachment to my instructor. He got me through a difficult challenge and changed my perspective on my capabilities.

Since then, I have been skydiving several more times. Now I cannot wait to step out of the plane. During each jump, I continue to be laser focused on safety and proper technique. At the same time, my enjoyment has substantially increased. I duplicated this mini-experiment for Japanese TV recently, taking blood before and after my fourth tandem skydive. This time, my stress hormones increased just 50 percent and my oxytocin went up by more than 200 percent. The challenge was surmountable and enjoyable. That is the power of eXpectation.

Here is the science. Stress is not bad. Full stop.

Chronic stress, the kind that weighs on your shoulders and never seems to dissipate, *is* bad. It leads to cardiovascular disease, depression, and diabetes. It also inhibits the release of oxytocin. But challenge stress is good for you. In fact, challenges are often fun. At least this is true for challenges that can be accomplished with sufficient effort and that conclude concretely. I knew my skydive would be over in 10 minutes. However scared I was, it had a clear end point (one way or another!).

Challenge stress causes our brains to block out distractions. When an important report is due, you skip replying to nonessential emails and reading gossipy news online. Your focus is on analysis and writing. The deep immersion in a project—often so much so that we lose track of time—has been called "flow" by my colleague Mihaly Csikszentmihalyi. Flow, Csikszentmihalyi has shown, is intrinsically rewarding. And it only occurs when one's objectives are clear.

During challenge stress, the brain directs the body to produce the fast-acting stress hormones epinephrine and adrenocorticotropin (ACTH). These produce hyperfocus and disconnect us from time. Unlike the neurochemicals evoked by unremitting chronic stress, the physiologic effects of challenge stress are shed rapidly after the challenge ends. When I drew my own blood after my first skydive, my hands were rock steady; the giddiness of the challenge had washed out of my nervous system by the time I floated to the ground.

It is important to have an Ovation after meeting eXpectations. After a goal is reached, celebrate the victory and have the team describe how they did it as part of the Ovation debrief. Supervisors should design eXpectations to generate small wins and then celebrate those wins. This sets up pathways in the brain that produce aspirations for the next win. After the goal is met and celebrated, let the team reset. The brain needs a refractory period after it has hyperfocused. As I mentioned in chapter 2, send the team to an amusement park or on some adventure together to enjoy being part of a successful team. Make it fun. Let the team have a few days of less-intense work before starting the next project. Make sure colleagues also catch up on sleep, family time, and recreation. This component of eXpectation can be summarized as challenge and recover.

Concrete and verifiable. For decades prior to 2007, teachers in Washington, D.C., regularly received superior reviews, even though many of their students could not read or write. In 2007, only 8 percent of eighth graders passed the grade-level competency exam in mathematics.[2] The schools performed poorly despite having the third-highest spending per student in the United States.[3] Desperate for change, Washington Mayor Adrian Fenty created a new position, education chancellor, that absorbed the power previously held by the Board of Education. Fenty hired education reformer Michelle Rhee as the first education chancellor in 2007. Rhee developed a teacher performance and evaluation instrument called IMPACT.

The first thing IMPACT did was provide "clear performance expectations" to teachers.[4] By setting concrete goals and a way to evaluate if these goals were being met, for the first time teachers received actionable feedback on their performance. This meant that principals could offer assistance, including instructional coaches, to those not reaching performance goals. The teachers' union agreed to a new contract with a 20 percent pay raise and performance bonuses of $20,000 to $30,000 in exchange for reduced job security. A total of 241 teachers who fell below performance goals were fired. In only three years, pass rates for the District of Columbia Comprehensive Assessment increased by 14 percentage points in reading and 17 in math.[5] Rhee made many other changes besides clarifying eXpectations, including closing nonperforming schools, adding early childhood education, expanding gifted-child classes, and providing additional music and art classes. The improvements in children's standardized test scores have been challenged by those who believe the data were falsified,[6] but setting attainable and concrete eXpectations is essential if colleagues are going to reach performance goals.

Then again, maybe the results in Washington were due to luck. Tennessee, a state scoring among the lowest in student achievement, would allow teachers to go up to 10 years between evaluations. About the same time Rhee was reforming Washington schools, Tennessee State Education Commissioner Kevin Huffman (Rhee's former husband) was implementing a similar program in his state. Teacher evaluations in Tennessee were not only related to student test scores but were tied to high eXpectations for teaching set by exemplar teachers. One cannot achieve excellence without knowing how excellence is measured.

Three years after setting eXpectations for teachers, Tennessee had the largest increase of any state on the 2013 National Assessment of Educational Progress. Tennessee fourth graders went from

46th in the nation in math to 37th; in reading they improved from 41st to 31st.[7] To be effective, eXpectations need to be specific, measurable, verifiable, and public.

eXpectation science. Stress has a nonlinear effect on oxytocin and trust. When epinephrine and ACTH increase moderately, they stimulate the brain to make oxytocin. Oxytocin motivates us to seek help from others to meet eXpectations. But like most things in biology, there is an inverted U curve relating physiological arousal to oxytocin. Without a challenge, there is no reason to produce oxytocin and reach out to others for help. On the other hand, when stress is overwhelming, the synthesis of oxytocin—and the desire to collaborate with others—is extinguished. Crushing stress puts us into survival mode where all we want to do is curl up in a ball and escape the insanity.

The skydive experiments I did on myself showed this effect: My first jump spiked stress hormones, resulting in only a small bump in oxytocin. By the time I took my fourth skydive, my stress response was moderate and my oxytocin surged. I was in sync with my skydive instructor, and we worked efficiently as a team. The same thing can happen at work. High-performance teams anticipate others' moves and respond effectively without having to articulate why they are doing what they are doing. These teams integrate new information deftly in order to reach a known objective. High-performance teams are also generative, improvising new solutions. For this to happen, though, team members have to trust each other.

Team size. The size of teams must be kept small if eXpectations are to be enforceable. Parkinson's law, "Work expands so as to fill the time available for its completion," holds always and everywhere. A corollary to Parkinson's law is known as the Ringelmann effect: Beyond a small team, the addition of coworkers causes a reduction in each team member's performance. You can stanch this motivation loss when team members are identified as individuals and eXpectations for each are clear.[8] Individual performance tends to level off when teams get larger than 6 to 12, varying by task type and objectives.[9] Many companies thrive by keeping team sizes small. At chemical and fabric maker W. L. Gore & Associates, manufacturing plants max out at 200 colleagues, and work groups stay in the single digits. The average team at Google has nine members.[10] At Spotify, the Stockholm-based music-streaming service, the fundamental organizing unit is a "squad," a five- to-seven-person team designed to function like an autonomous start-up. Each squad has a specific mission and focus.

Enterprise Rent-A-Car opens a new location when an existing outlet reaches 150 rental cars. Typical Enterprise locations have a maximum of eight colleagues. Those at a branch know their colleagues well and can support them when seeking to reach eXpectations. Branch managers at Enterprise are empowered to determine fleet size, open new branches, and sell used cars. In essence, Enterprise views each location as an independent business and gives managers the freedom to sustain profitability.[11] *BusinessWeek* magazine identified Enterprise as one of the best places to begin a career because of the autonomy managers have.[12] Enterprise is now the largest rental car company in the United States, with 68,000 employees and annual revenues exceeding $18 billion.

Building team eXpectations. Team performance is highest when everyone has a say in how work is done. Encourage junior colleagues to contribute in a toss-out-some-ideas approach. Also make sure you include, when possible, an equal number of men and women. Many research studies in psychology and management show that decision quality and creative problem solving are better in mixed-gender groups and groups that mix personality types. Include introverts and extroverts, as well as those who think before they talk and those who blurt things out rapidly. A diverse team has a higher team IQ than the average IQ of the team's members.[13]

When building teams, spend the first hour having members get to know each other. Start with names and job titles. I like to have people tell others something weird about themselves. It makes that person's name easier to remember. For example, in a graduate class years ago, a student named Jason told me he had huge toes. Of course, I asked to see his toes, and everyone in the room laughed with him when he took off his shoes. I still remember him. Sharing personal or even embarrassing things builds camaraderie and empathy between team members.

The next step is to write a script for the project. The script outlines short-term and long-term goals, and details who does what when. This provides an eXpectation checklist so the team leader and all team members can see the progress they are making. The script also allows everyone to identify when the project gets stuck and to seek extra help if needed. Checklists are used by pilots before taking off, nuclear power plant technicians, and, increasingly, doctors and surgeons treating patients. They are an effective way to ensure quality and measure progress.

Action challenges. For organizations that work on a per-project basis, the length of the project determines when the challenge is over. This can be the date the project is completed or when a specified amount of work has been done, but it must be clear to all. Post this on a flip chart or write it on a whiteboard. Make sure everyone is focused on hitting the goal. For organizations in which the workload is roughly constant, set eXpectations in terms of actions, not outcomes. "Speak to five prospective customers every day this week" or "Call one former client every day and say hello." These are achievable goals that require action. Get creative and move eXpectations around so that goals do not get stale. If goals are met too easily, push them up, sometimes way up, for a week or two.

Oxytocin release is stimulated when eXpectations are cast as group challenges. This is an effective way to build trust among team members. Think of the military: The difficult training and deployment soldiers face form powerful bonds among "bands of brothers." Challenges at work have a similar effect. They cannot be too easy, but also not impossible. The goal of eXpectation is to design challenges that are, well, challenging.

Coaching for eXpectations. When I took my 11-year-old daughter snow skiing for the first time, during her first run on the intermediate trail she fell hard and skinned her knuckles on some ice. She cried and did not want to continue skiing. Over her protestations, I made her get back on the lift. She had to try one more time. On the next run, she made it all the way without falling and was beaming when she got to the bottom. She had mastered this difficult task and felt great about what she had done. And of course, she wanted to do it again. The brain's reward circuit activates when we triumph over difficult challenges. This creates a desire to take on another challenge and get the reward for it.

Teresa Amabile at Harvard Business School analyzed 12,000 diary entries of employees in a variety of industries. She found that making progress toward one's goals was the most important motivator at work. Fully 76 percent of people's best days at work occurred when they fulfilled eXpectations. She also found that 43 percent of good days at work occurred when team members helped others. Almost by accident, Amabile also discovered that when colleagues progressed toward goals, their moods improved. This is just what neuroscience experiments on eXpectations show: It is enjoyable to triumph over a challenge. And because moods are contagious, when one colleague or team meets an eXpectation, it gives a bliss boost to others.[14] Meeting eXpectations can produce Joy at work.

Once concrete eXpectations are set, weekly feedback from supervisors is necessary. Breaking eXpectations into weekly milestones allows leaders to assess when additional resources, people, or training are needed to reach goals. Weekly meetings should be approached from a coaching perspective (more on that in chapter 4). I like to ask, "What can I do to help you reach your goal?" Often, the answers surprise me. They range from, "I'm good" to "I can't do this project" to "My team is not working effectively." When problems arise, immediate action is necessary to remove bottlenecks and continue forward progress.

I also recommend a daily huddle. "How's your project going?" and "Can I do anything to help?" are key questions. Many businesses, such as The Container Store, the natural-cleaning-products company Method, Capital One, and Ritz-Carlton, do daily check-ins using a stand-up huddle. This keeps meetings short and focused on the most important topics. If colleagues need help or guidance on a project, the supervisor knows it rapidly and can provide the necessary resources if possible. The focus should be on hot projects—what needs to be done today—and lessons from yesterday. In daily huddles, make eye contact and ban all electronics unless team members are at different locations. The focus should be on "we," not "I" or "you." Huddles reinforce eXpectations.

You should resist the temptation to constantly adjust eXpectations midproject. Pivots are fine, but multiple radical changes induce chronic stress and disengagement. Supervisors must set clear, challenging, and obtainable eXpectations and serve as coaches to team members.

eXpectation alignment. A simple and transparent way to follow up on eXpectations is to use the assessment technique known as "Start,

Stop, Continue." At your weekly all-hands meeting, assess the progress toward the goal, its importance to your organization's strategy, and the likelihood of attaining the goal. This simple metric captures Bayesian updating, the mathematical system that incorporates new information into decision processes. Sometimes an inability to hit weekly milestones is a sign that a project should be stopped before it is completed. If the team is not making progress, and if you have truly invested effort to move it forward, then it may be better to pull the plug now rather than keep going. Many companies, including Netflix, consistently use Start, Stop, Continue to assess projects.

If team members decide a project should be continued, but it faces a serious bottleneck, changing the team leader or swapping out team members can restore momentum. For many reasons, a team's best efforts sometimes do not produce results. When teams are regularly formed and reformed, colleagues expect to change work groups regularly. This is a valuable way to cross-train individuals, and it invests in their professional growth (more on this in chapter 8). Colleagues need to understand that the project they are working on contributes to the entire organization's success, not simply their own goals. If the project is not moving forward, then the organization is weakened and changes must be made.

The ability to set clear eXpectations, deliver feedback, and provide Ovation when goals are met can be facilitated using a number of software products such as Halogen Performance, SuccessFactors, or Cornerstone Performance. These remind key colleagues to set eXpectations, coach team members, and do weekly one-on-ones. They also increase Openness (see chapter 6) by connecting a colleague's individual goals to the organization's objectives. These automated solutions remove the need to remember all the tasks one has to do and provide virtual feedback as often as it is needed. They also require leaders to make eXpectations concrete and state the milestones needed to achieve success. General Electric created an app called PD@GE for "performance development at GE" to help supervisors guide direct reports. Managers are expected to have frequent touch-point discussions with colleagues, coaching them toward meeting goals and getting feedback themselves. Unlike the old days at GE, this management approach is focused on positive reinforcement rather than fear.[15]

Overwork diminishes performance. Carefully monitor colleagues for signs of chronic stress and intervene if you see it. Such signs include excessive hours in the office, weight gain or loss, disengagement from others, and a high volume of emails sent in the middle of the night. This is where weekly team meetings and one-on-ones are necessary. If you suspect chronic stress, ask about it. Suggest time off to recover. Additional people or resources can be brought in to relieve a stressed-out colleague. eXpectations that are vague or unachievable provoke chronic stress and inhibit coordinated teamwork.

Boston Consulting Group developed an alert for chronic stress it calls the red zone. If a colleague averages more than 60 work hours over five weeks, a red card is sent to that person's supervisor. If the heavy workload is temporary, the supervisor checks in and the card is removed. If overwork is a consistent pattern, the supervisor sends some projects to others and helps the colleague keep work hours reasonable. Boston Consulting's approach recognizes that to complete projects, sometimes long hours are necessary. But to keep the best people and have them work optimally, challenge stress should not morph into chronic stress.

Pygmalion effect. The desire to meet a socially stated goal is known as the Pygmalion effect. A classic study had supervisors tell randomly chosen employees that they were "superior," increasing eXpectations about their performance. Evaluations by independent raters 3 to 12 months later showed that an unusually large number of these average employees actually became superior. Studies of officer candidates for the Israeli Defense Forces and the U.S. Navy, and employees in heavy industry, confirm the Pygmalion effect works.[16] Across these studies, 12 to 17 percent of average employees performed at a superior level due to the Pygmalion effect. Researchers have shown that high performers also raise the performance of those around them, increasing the power of challenging eXpectations.

Some companies set eXpectations through job titles. Taco Bell calls its food preparers Food Champions, and cashiers are Service Champions. Disney has Imagineers and Cast Members; Starbucks has Partners, and, of course, Apple has Geniuses. This approach connects a colleague's identity with the eXpectation of excellence. "What do you do?" "I'm an Apple Genius." An employee with such a title needs to provide the best service or risk embarrassment. I interviewed a 20-year Cast Member at Disneyland whose job was to sweep up trash. I asked him if he enjoyed working for Disney. He told me he "gets to make people happy every day" and looks forward to coming to work, even after 20 years. Disney's mission to be the "Happiest Place on Earth" is internalized by setting eXpectations that visitors will be as happy as humanly possible.

The opposite effect also holds. It has been called the Golem effect. If leaders explicitly or implicitly signal that team members are incompetent or lazy, it is no surprise that people tend to underperform. I worked at a gas station in high school and during my first week I asked another employee what I should be doing when there were no customers. His answer? "Cool your heels." That is just what I did. If eXpectations are set low, they, too, will be fulfilled.

Training and trust are the ingredients that feed the Pygmalion effect. Simply saying "You are wonderful" will not do it. But giving colleagues high eXpectations and the ability to reach them is the way to marshal the neurological foundations of intrinsic motivation. Ovation reinforces eXpectation and engages the brain's learning circuit in a feedback loop.

eXpectation turnarounds. The Royal Bank of Canada used eXpectations to improve performance during its 2004–05 turnaround. By 2004, Canada's largest bank was lagging, both structurally and financially. Decisions took eons to make, and collaboration between business units was rare. CEO Gordon Nixon engineered a series of culture changes to align the bank's execution with its goals. One of the first things he did was to set concrete eXpectations for all business units. Across the bank's businesses, joint goals were established so that units would work together to meet organization-wide objectives. To put teeth into eXpectations, each unit wrote a charter so that eXpectations and accountability were transparent (the importance of transparency is discussed in chapter 6). A key charter component was welcoming challenges rather than avoiding them. These changes worked. By 2007, Royal Bank colleagues were focused on meeting eXpectations, and its financial performance was best in class.

Toyota has been able to change eXpectations and thereby dramatically increase output. General Motors had an assembly plant in Fremont, California, that for years had low productivity, made low-quality vehicles, and faced recurrent strikes. Unable to resolve these problems, GM closed the plant in 1982. According to the United Automobile Workers union, GM's Fremont employees were "considered the worst workforce in the automobile industry in the United States."[17]

Toyota began a collaboration with GM in the 1980s, and the Fremont plant was reopened under Toyota management and christened NUMMI (New United Motor Manufacturing Inc.). Most of the former GM workers were rehired and trained in the Toyota

Production System. This was the first Toyota manufacturing facility in North America and the first time Toyota's continuous-improvement system was translated to a non-Japanese setting. According to Toyota documents, executives were skeptical that Americans would be able to use Toyota's system.

Concrete eXpectations for quality and productivity were set, and everyone knew that the plant would only remain open if they were met. Rather than resist these goals, workers embraced them. Absenteeism fell from close to 20 percent under GM's management to 2 percent after Toyota took over. Toyota managers showed they trusted employees by allowing them to stop the production line whenever a defect was found. A key Toyota value is "Respect for People," putting colleagues first. For example, GM regularly laid off employees when sales fell, but Toyota committed to making cuts elsewhere, including in supervisors' pay, before laying off employees. Across all their duties, managers were required to follow through on their commitments, building mutual trust.[18]

The culture of high eXpectations at NUMMI reduced the assembly time of a car from 31 hours at a typical GM plant to 19 hours. GM had an average defect rate of 135 per 100 cars produced. At NUMMI, the defect rate was 45 per 100 cars.[19] High eXpectations and continuous feedback between employees and supervisors were the keys to the turnaround. Indeed, supervisors celebrated when assembly-line colleagues pulled an *andon* (a hanging cord) to stop the production line and fix a problem.

Building a culture of trust means that all colleagues are accountable for their assignments. Accountability is implemented through eXpectation. If assignments are missed, leaders need to know why and seek to ensure this pattern is not repeated.

Pay and eXpectation. You may have noticed that I have not linked pay to eXpectation. This is deliberate. A recent survey showed that supervisors believe that 89 percent of employees leave because of pay. The actual number of employees who leave for a higher salary: 12 percent. Work is not about pay. People need a paycheck, but they do not put their passion into work because of money.

As much as possible, you should dissociate pay from performance. Research by Kathleen Vohs and colleagues at the University of Minnesota showed that just thinking about money substantially reduces cooperation. Building a high-trust culture harnesses individuals' intrinsic motivation to meet goals as a social endeavor. Its call to action is, "We are all in this together."

Measuring the contributions made by individual team members is important in determining if eXpectations were met, but the organization's success requires that individuals work effectively as teams. Team members themselves are often an effective source of value-creation information, using, for example, 360 evaluations. But to reinforce the importance of cooperation, salary revisions should depend on the success of the entire organization. This approach contravenes the you-eat-what-you-kill salary structure that uses purely monetary motivations for work. Using team eXpectations, with the understanding that high performance permits additional compensation, mobilizes colleagues' implicit and explicit motivation.

It turns out that even a modest amount of pay for performance crowds out implicit motivation. We discovered this in an experiment in my lab run by then postdoctoral researcher Veronika Alexander. She measured neurologic activity while participants did a work task 40 times. Participants were assigned to one of three treatments: They were paid 50 cents, 75 cents, or $1 for each correctly completed task. Next came the provocative part of the experiment. She told participants that most people would earn $20 for completing the study. Some quick math shows that this means that the lowest piece-rate group had to solve every problem correctly to earn the average pay. Compare this to the middle pay group, which only had to complete 70 percent correctly to hit the average, while the highest paid group only needed to finish 50 percent to earn the average pay.

If pay is too low, motivation lags. This is like the 1980s supermodel Linda Evangelista who famously said, "I don't even get out of bed for less than $10,000." On the other hand, paying people a lot of money for each task motivates them to just do it for the money rather than because it is intrinsically rewarding to complete a task.

Who performed the best? The middle pay group got 72 percent correct, while the low- and high-pay groups correctly completed 63 and 64 percent. The neurologic data showed why. Arousal, as measured by heart rate, was highest in the low- and high-pay groups, but moderate for those who got the middle piece rate. These data show that the low-pay participants were stressed out trying to reach the nearly impossible goal of perfection. They were overchallenged, trying to meet unrealistic eXpectations. Those in the high-pay group were also overstressed, but for a different reason. They were all about explicit motivation: With a lot of money on the line, they tried to work extra hard to get it. The high pay inhibited their performance as they tried to dip into the pot of gold. Those who received moderate pay seemed to balance the implicit motivation of completing a challenge and the explicit motivation of receiving a decent paycheck. Their arousal was moderate and performance high.

Studies throughout psychology and biology have found this same "Goldilocks" result: Too little is not good, nor is too much. This is known as the Yerkes-Dodson law and traces out an inverted U curve. The sweet spot is found in the middle: Challenge colleagues on projects and pay them a fair wage to work. This captures implicit and explicit motivation. This sweet-spot approach matches the inverted U response of oxytocin to challenge stress discussed earlier in this chapter. And therein lies the art of eXpectation: setting challenges that are difficult but attainable while volunteer-employees are paid fairly. Expect to have to continually tweak both these factors.

The exception to avoiding pay-to-play schemes is unexpected bonuses. As part of Ovation, bonuses paid to colleagues who complete projects early or under budget are warranted and can be excellent motivators. But if bonuses are expected for every project completed, then explicit motivation rules and the social motivation of teamwork is inhibited.

Termination. Sometimes intrinsic and extrinsic motivation are not enough. When eXpectations are continually missed and remediation strategies have not improved a colleague's ability to reach eXpectations, then the colleague and other team members are frustrated. Weekly one-on-ones should discuss why eXpectations continue to be missed. Saying, "You seem to have trouble meeting your goals. How can I help?" is a way to start. When this does not work, I start to discuss how this position does not seem to be working out and how I can help the colleague find a more appropriate job. When eXpectations are clear, no one should be surprised when a colleague has to be let go. If the team member has sincerely tried to do the job for which he or she was hired, I use my network to help that person find a new position. This is the long game: We might do a project together at the new company, or we might hire the person back later to work for us after additional training. My objective when I let someone go is for that person to offer to take me to lunch: The colleague has been frustrated by the inability to meet eXpectations, and I'm going to resolve that frustration. Everyone should be happy about that.

Gaming eXpectation. During the yearlong Soviet blockade of Berlin (1948–49), volunteers unloaded planeloads of food and supplies from the West day and night. Maj. Gen. William H. Tunner commanded the operation. The daily grind quickly caused morale and performance to lag. To combat this, Tunner set daily eXpectations in the form of a contest. Teams would compete to unload the planes fastest. All teams celebrated the winners together with a fine meal. This earned General Tunner the nickname "tonnage Tunner." He changed the mundane into a game.

Gamification of work is an increasingly popular way to set eXpectations. While some view this as a modern and pernicious version of Taylorism, many organizations that have gamified tasks have seen greater focus and engagement. The core idea of gamification is that work should be like playing Candy Crush Saga, with clear goals followed by Ovations for reaching milestones. As discussed in chapter 2, the amount of Zollars earned by Zappos.com employees quantifies a task's importance for which help was received. This is a simple version of gamification.

Gamification is most fruitfully used in training and certification programs. Training often includes significant periods of mandated knowledge transfer that can be a potent soporific. If, instead, reaching levels of expertise is fun, then training can be made more engaging, and colleagues may look forward to it.[20] Today, 70 percent of Forbes Global 2000 companies use gamification to increase colleague engagement.[21] Experiments run by faculty from the University of Pennsylvania's Wharton School have shown that gamification improves mood but not necessarily productivity. They discovered an important caveat: Colleagues must voluntarily opt into the game to get a mood boost. Forced gamification is like forced anything—it ceases to be fun.[22]

The dark side of gamification comes from the desire by some organizations to incentivize microtasks. This approach to gamification can inhibit flexibility and creativity. An equally important issue is the lack of control employees have in fully gamified businesses.

The control from above of one's work life ignores the fluid nature of modern business. It is a short step from microtasks to micromanagement. The antidote to micromanagement of colleagues is the topic of chapter 4.

☕ MONDAY MORNING LIST

▶ Break eXpectations into difficult but achievable weekly actions.

▶ Create a challenge board showing eXpectations for teams.

▶ Train leaders to become coaches who use daily huddles and one-on-ones.

▶ Vary challenges from easy to hard.

▶ When goals are reached, orchestrate Ovation and a post-project debrief.

Chapter 4

Yield

Yield occurs when colleagues choose how to do a project. Yield explains 51 percent of organizational trust.

You're the boss. You understand everything about your organization. If not, you wouldn't be in charge. As a result, you are the go-to-person in every situation.

If this sounds familiar, then a problem is brewing. When a leader solves all the organization's problems (which are, often, people problems), she or he often cannot focus on a leader's most important job: designing and implementing strategies so the organization flourishes in the long term. Compounding this mistake, micromanagement also removes the opportunity for colleagues to "own" a project by allowing them to choose how it is done. We learned in chapter 3 that individuals perform best when they are given challenges and receive feedback at least weekly. Let's take this idea to its logical conclusion: Why not hourly feedback? That is micromanagement of the Taylorism variety, and it fails because it removes colleagues' ability to control their destinies. It also fails because it restricts colleagues from doing anything other than the typical routine.

A 2014 Citigroup survey found that nearly half of employees would give up a 20 percent raise for greater Yield.[1] The demand for Yield is there; what are you doing about it? This chapter shows you how to enable Yield while maintaining clear eXpectations.

In 2005, a Wisconsin manufacturing facility that produced industrial automation equipment was going bankrupt. Even though it had a solid customer base in a niche market, its profitability was uneven. Later that year, it was purchased by Barry-Wehmiller Companies, a business we read about in chapter 2. The Wisconsin facility would complement Barry-Wehmiller's existing portfolio of companies but was poorly managed.

The plant was closed while the new management settled in. The first thing leaders did was to hold an all-hands meeting to introduce themselves and announce their objectives. Current employees were to be retained, and the company would keep its name and location in its small community. Barry-Wehmiller wanted to change the culture to secure consistent profitability. The new managers asked employees to describe the strengths and weaknesses of their company. One by one they spoke while managers took notes. The queue reached a machinist I'll call Joe who had worked there 27 years. Joe was in his mid-50s and knew his job well. As he related numerous ways that production could be made more efficient, he started to cry.

The room fell silent as Joe composed himself. He said that after working at the company for a year, he had made some of these suggestions to his foreman. He had found that a couple of steps could be cut out of the production process for one product. "Could we make these changes?" Joe asked his foreman. The foreman told him, "We don't pay you to think, you're just a pair of hands. Get back to the line." Joe never made another suggestion. Twenty-six years later, someone finally wanted to listen to Joe about processes he new intimately well.[2]

Inclusion and diversity. Yield is the antidote to the vestige of Taylorism that pervades many organizations. When colleagues have the appropriate training and experience to complete a project, Yield allows them to fully commit to eXpectations by taking ownership of the execution and outcomes. Inevitably, a colleague will execute the project slightly differently than a supervisor would have. As long as the project is completed and catastrophic failures do not occur, this should be celebrated.

Setting eXpectations is absolutely necessary so objectives are clear. When, in addition, colleagues are trusted with Yield, small innovations naturally occur. Former Gucci Group CEO Robert Polet calls this "freedom within the framework."[3] It means that colleagues try new ideas out and learn from others in the organization, especially those from different divisions. Former General Electric CEO Jack Welch has called this a "boundaryless company," where innovation occurs consistently and is shared broadly.

Yield is an evolutionary process, it embodies variation and selection. eXpectations are set to be difficult but achievable to stimulate innovation, and Yield permits variation in how goals are met. The "selection" part of the evolutionary process occurs during Ovation when wins are celebrated and how the team achieved the win is shared. The debrief needs to be formally recorded and communicated to all interested parties so others can imitate innovations. If the team hits its goal the same way as before, that's fine if processes are effective and efficient. Sometimes good enough is good enough. The United States Aviation Safety Reporting System is credited, in part, with reducing airline accidents by 95 percent, going from 0.053 per 100,000 miles flown in 1975 to 0.0025 in 2008, by reducing the variation in how planes are flown. When airline accidents do occur, they provide a tableau through which industry standards can be improved. Execution failures at work provide the same learning opportunity.

Celebrate mistakes. One of the most famous management experiments occurred from 1924 to 1932 at the Hawthorne Works, a Western Electric equipment manufacturing plant in Cicero, Illinois. Industrial psychologists observed colleagues and measured productivity while they made small changes in lighting, shift length, and break times. They found that nearly every change, including a return to the status quo, improved productivity. Most scholars view these findings as inducing an observer effect, often called the Hawthorne effect, in which just having someone watch what people are doing at work improves outcomes. As social creatures, we enjoy being part of a group worthy of attention, so we work just a little harder. The Ovation debrief induces a type of Hawthorne effect: Tracking mistakes reduces them, and embracing improvements reinforces their future use.

Mistakes are mitigated by training (formal and from peers) and oversight. Risk-management backstops must be maintained at all times. Nevertheless, mistakes are going to happen. Mistakes can even be a reason for Ovation. Many organizations—for example, experience designer Surprise Industries, Ben & Jerry's ice cream, Daruma Capital Management, and software maker Valve Corp.— have regular Ovations celebrating mistakes and, importantly, what was learned from them. How about starting a "Congratulations, you messed up!" Ovation once a month? Fail fast and fail often. Then lick your wounds and move on to innovate again. Herb Kelleher, founder of Southwest Airlines, once observed, "You build self-confidence when you give people the room to take risks and you give them the room to fail. You don't condemn them when they fail, you just say, 'that's an educational experience.'"[4] Professional networking company LinkedIn considers new ventures by discussing previous failures. It defines "intelligent risk" as having a 3× upside, a sufficient likelihood of hitting the upside, and a fit to its portfolio of other risky projects. Intelligent risks are smart to take.

If eXpectations have been established, then supervisors are receiving formal feedback weekly from team members. This can be supplemented by daily huddles that facilitate Yield. Just like the huddle used in sports, a supervisor's role in a high Yield organization is akin to a coach or counselor rather than an omniscient dictator. See a reason for a change? Call an audible and let the coach know. Sometimes this results in an improvement and sometimes it fails. The best learning is learning through (small) mistakes because such experiences are encoded more powerfully in the brain than when we are simply told a new fact. Without mistakes there is no innovation. You should train intensively and delegate generously.

Free to choose. The Soviet Union failed for many reasons, but two are prominent. First, the system of governance was inconsistent with human nature: People want to have a say in how their society is run. The second failure was in the design of its economic system. Information flowed in one direction, from the top leaders and their Five Year Plans to supposedly enthusiastic Soviet workers. Enthusiasm for the Soviet system quickly waned, so Stalin and his successors created a police state that compelled compliance. In a similar way, managers who compel compliance fall into the same traps: They ignore the human desire for autonomy and they limit bottom-up information flows that Yield enables.

The manufacturing plant Barry-Wehmiller purchased in Wisconsin was a police state before it was bought. White-shirted managers determined what to make and how it would be made. Blue-shirted employees were treated as drones who would goldbrick if not monitored constantly. The white shirts absolutely knew that the blue shirts would steal materials if given the chance. Prior to the purchase by Barry-Wehmiller, a locked metal gate blocked the entrance to the spare-parts room. If colleagues needed a part, they had to find a manager to unlock the gate and be escorted in and out of the room. Remember, this is a manufacturing plant; spare parts were needed nearly every day. Not only did this system cause production delays, it sent an obvious we-don't-trust-you message to colleagues.

One of the first things Barry-Wehmiller did was to remove the locked gate. The new managers made it clear that everyone was in the same boat: If this company was going to survive, everyone had to pull together as volunteer-employees to increase efficiency. Need a part? Get it. Have an idea to improve productivity? Give it a try.

Yield empowers colleagues with choice, an essential component to innovation. It also means that colleagues are going to make mistakes. And that is where things get complicated. Unless people try to do things differently, improvements will not be discovered. But often a leader's ability to accept mistakes as part of the learning process is difficult. Therein lies the tension: A desire for a no-mistakes workplace is anathema to a culture of innovation. Those doing the work often see things that those in the penthouse do not. Peter Drucker wrote, "Improvement starts with feedback from the front line."

Innovation is not only inhibited by task rigidity, but also by how leaders respond to changes. Even though we say that people learn through mistakes, in most organizations mistakes are punished, implicitly or explicitly. A culture that responds appropriately to mistakes affects how the brain encodes new information and whether it will be a source of innovation or not. The brain recognizes a mistake first by activating an alert system that releases a squirt of dopamine deep in the brain stem. This chemical signal tells us to pay attention.

Dopamine next produces activation in a frontal brain region called the anterior cingulate cortex that says, "Something is wrong with my theory of the world." The pattern the brain expected to see did not occur—that is how the brain recognizes a mistake. The next time one does this task, it will be completed more slowly while we test our revised theory of how "A" causes "B."

This is where culture comes in. The dopamine circuit compels us to learn from mistakes. If the boss starts yelling after an error, the mistake-recognition system in the brain equates mistakes with punishment. The result is easy to foresee: Colleagues hide mistakes to avoid punishment. Instead, if the boss congratulates you on identifying a mistake or trying something new that failed, the learning circuit produces a positive association between mistakes and social recognition. Creating a culture that embraces and celebrates learning through mistakes directly impacts the brain's motivation to innovate by encoding deviations from the norm as pleasurable and enhancing their recall.

Experiments that have varied the degree of oversight of employees confirm that micromanagement inhibits innovation. A study that assigned casino employees to either "tight" or "loose" supervision found that constant monitoring inhibited learning and innovation. In fact, no innovation occurred at all with tight monitoring by supervisors.[5]

Jeff Bezos, CEO of Amazon.com, encourages his colleagues to learn through mistakes while accepting that many attempts at improvement fail. "If you're going to take bold bets, they're going to be experiments," he has said. "And if they're experiments you don't know ahead of time if they're going to work. Experiments are by their very nature prone to failure. But a few big successes compensate for dozens and dozens of things that didn't work. . . . I've made billions of dollars of failures at Amazon.com."[6]

The "try it out" notion is essential to Yield. Front-line colleagues have the most extensive information about what they are doing, and Yield empowers them to innovate. Indeed, almost all innovation comes from those doing the job. A Harvard Business School analysis of companies like Pixar that consistently innovate found that all of them had cultures of high Yield.[7] Experimentation and learning occur at much higher rates when colleagues are empowered to challenge the status quo. Businesses using coercion to try to mandate innovation are unlikely to get it. Innovation is fundamentally antiauthoritarian and only arises with Yield.

Yield in teams. In my lab we implement Yield by using people's names. Each project has a "Primary," or leader. This is the same approach used in the Toyota Production System in which the Primary is the chief engineer, or *shusa*. For each new project, the Primary is named publicly, and we build teams around that person. Primaries take ownership of projects and run them as they see fit. Supervisors set clear eXpectations and provide Primaries with feedback in a weekly all-hands meeting and daily huddles, allocating people and resources as needed. Innovation is encouraged, and small mistakes are celebrated. When the project is complete, we organize an Ovation to celebrate the win. During the Ovation we debrief to see what went right, what went wrong, and what others can learn from the team's experience.

As discussed in chapter 2, debriefs need to occur shortly after a project ends so that the brain associates experiences during the project with outcomes achieved. The challenge stress of being part of a team stimulates the release of oxytocin and promotes effective teamwork.

This approach is used in a variety of high-stakes organizations. I spent a day embedded with the U.S. Army during training exercises deep in the mountains of southern California, and I was impressed with the balance the soldiers achieved between Yield and mistake minimization. After every simulated assault, there was an immediate debrief. All soldiers, regardless of rank, and even the visiting academic, were asked what they saw. The commander asked for three things that were done right and three things done wrong. No fingers were pointed; the discussions focused on how to execute more effectively in a fluid environment. War veterans used their experiences in battle to add gravity to the debrief.

Generating and testing new ideas. Neuroscience tells us why innovation is more likely to occur during challenges. It turns out that the brain is a very stingy organ. It makes up about 3 percent of body weight but takes 20 percent of your caloric metabolism to run. The brain manages this high overhead rate by seeking to automate tasks it does repeatedly. This is why you can drive your car and at the same time hold a conversation, listen to the radio, and answer the phone. Driving has been automated, until, that is, the car in front of you hits its brakes and you need to put all your attentional resources into avoiding a collision. Yield allows colleagues to drive the car, and when leaders set challenging eXpectations identifies the destination and the speed needed to get there. When the project has to pivot because the brake lights come on, cognitive resources are marshaled more effectively than when employees are mindlessly following orders.

Yes, Yield requires more effort than simply business as usual. But it also marshals more cognitive resources, a phenomenon called effort justification. A 1959 experiment by the psychologists Elliot Aronson of Stanford University and Judson Mills of the U.S. Army found that people who had to go through an embarrassing situation before joining a discussion group later reported being more connected to group members. A follow-up study that would never be done today gave electric shocks to participants randomly formed into groups. Those who received the strongest shocks reported that they valued their group more than those who got mild shocks. Working hard as a team under high eXpectations is the "shock" of being fully engaged at work. Set hard but achievable eXpectations, and then cut the team loose.

One of the great experimenters of all time was Leonardo da Vinci. He was able to innovate in many domains by trying new things and evaluating the outcomes. Yield allows everyone in your organization to be a da Vinci. To systematize innovation, da Vinci developed seven principles of discovery. One of these he called *dimostrazione.* This is a commitment to test knowledge through experience and learn from mistakes. If this is good enough for da Vinci . . . well, you get the point. Yield allows individuals to test process improvements constantly with limited downside. If a new approach does not produce an improvement, then return to the status quo.

Youthful innovation. Often younger and less-experienced colleagues are your chief innovators. You know how many dumb things you did when you were young, but some of them paid off. Now that you are older and wiser, you probably make fewer positive and negative deviations from what is expected. Empower younger colleagues to experiment and see what happens, because the "experts" do not always have the most innovative ideas. Case in point: In 2004, the U.S. Congress mandated that by 2015 one-third of military ground vehicles had to be autonomous. Initially, established automobile manufacturers were funded to produce autonomous vehicles. After five years and significant investment by the government, no progress had been made. Changing tack, the Defense Advanced Research Projects Agency offered all comers a $1 million prize for a self-driving car that could complete a course in the Mojave Desert in less than 10 hours. Two years later, a group of engineering students from Stanford University won the challenge. They beat a team from Carnegie Mellon University by a mere 11 minutes. In a similar vein, in 2012, two University of Toronto graduate students were the first to produce sustained flight in a human-powered helicopter; established engineers were convinced a human-powered helicopter was impossible. These young people broke rules they did not even know existed to create spectacular breakthroughs.

Incremental improvements are made when one uses single-loop learning. This approach improves a process or product by refining existing techniques. Radical improvements come from double-loop learning in which the underlying assumptions about the mechanisms producing results are questioned and sometimes discarded. Double-loop learning even questions the reasons why an innovation is needed, asking, "Why are we doing this?," rather than "How do we improve this?.[8] Young people, who are less wedded to tradition, may be better at double-loop learning and thus at creating significant innovations.[9]

Yield provides the space for double-loop learning. High-trust cultures permit core business processes to be challenged, even if they have worked well in the past or were established by the founders. You can implement Yield by using objective data to determine improvements and disseminating findings organization-wide. What's right is right. Colleagues can tweak the existing operating model, or they can throw the model out and try to materially accelerate performance. The latter is more likely when Yield is high.

Inclusion and empowerment. A classic study compared U.S. naval units classified as "average" and "superior." No differences were found in commitment, processes, or command structure. But average units had commanding officers who acted like autocrats. The essence of autocratic management is, "Do this because I say so." Superior naval commands were more open to innovation, with commanding officers who listened to, and took, advice from others.[10]

A similar effect occurs in the classroom. Between 40 and 50 percent of teachers leave the profession within five years of starting their careers. A teacher interviewed about why he quit said, "Teachers in schools do not call the shots. They have very little say. They're told what to do; it's a very disempowered line of work.[11] It is no surprise that many teachers are disengaged; it is Taylorism rearing its head again.

Luxury hotelier Ritz-Carlton, twice the recipient of the prestigious Malcolm Baldrige National Quality Award, Yields authority to its "Ladies" and "Gentlemen" (wonderful eXpectation titles), from bellhop to desk clerk, to spend up to $2,000 to fix any customer's problem. Supervisors do not question these expenditures. The Ritz-Carlton has successfully created a culture of trusting colleagues to create extraordinary experiences for their guests.

Micromanagement not only erodes trust, it erodes health as well. Direction from above causes people to lose their "locus of control," or sense of command over their lives. When locus of control is high, intrinsic motivation soars and job satisfaction rises.[12] Maintaining control of one's work life is essential to good physical and mental health (evidence for this is in chapter 11). Yield invites full participation by everyone, from janitors to customer service representatives. The information is out there; it just needs to be liberated.

Yield and customer service. Colleagues in high-Yield organizations enjoy the process of work because they control how it is done. I consulted for a large pharmacy benefits manager as it rapidly grew. An ongoing issue was keeping the call center fully staffed with trained agents. During one visit, I spoke to a call center colleague who had worked the phones for 20 years. "Why," I asked, "haven't you accepted a promotion?" She told me that every day she was happy because she helped people get the medicine they needed. The company had high Yield in the call center, giving agents substantial discretion to help their customers. "I don't want a different job," she told me. The good feeling of helping people in a company with Yield kept her satisfied with her job.

Online retailer Zappos is a high-Yield company. Phone representatives are lauded for spending hours with customers who are in a pickle. Zappos agents can even send gifts like flowers or chocolates to customers who have good and bad experiences without getting a supervisor's permission to do so. Because Zappos's customer-loyalty reps can stay on calls with a customer as long as they want, service is extraordinary. A Zappos colleague was recently on a call for more than 10 hours.[13] This level of service would be impossible without Yield.

How do you go from a command-and-control structure to one with Yield? Start small. For example, implement Yield in one department. An insurance-services company I worked with had very uneven Ofactor scores across divisions. A particularly low-trust division was in insurance claims. Turnover was 100 percent annually, and trust was very low. Its Yield was at the 30th percentile. I recommended that rather than try to script claims agents' conversations with their customers, limiting what they could do, Yield would be increased when agents were given greater discretion in making decisions. "Let me check with my supervisor" frustrates agent and customer. Yield trusts colleagues to engage with customers as they see fit. It can even strengthen the attachment colleagues have for the organization.

A Yield experiment at a large office-equipment supplier was shown to increase colleague commitment to the corporation. The company empowered customer service engineers to organize their work assignments themselves, to choose whether to repair or replace equipment, and to complete assignments using processes as they saw fit. Customer service engineers work in small teams, and the selection of team members was also devolved to the team level. This approach increased commitment to the organization by 23 percent compared to command-and-control management.[14]

Crowd sourcing innovation. Yield sparks innovation by drawing on the wisdom of front-line colleagues. The multinational Indian software services company HCL Technologies realized that good ideas can come from any part of the company, so it created an online portal called iGen on the company's intranet. This site allowed colleagues to submit ideas on any topic, from business development to new products to administrative streamlining to new learning opportunities for team members. HCL experimented with many of these ideas, eventually implementing about 25 percent of them. The online suggestion box was so successful that HCL began holding innovation contests in which teams presented their approaches to problems for possible implementation. With so many suggestions, HCL decided to crowdsource the identification of the best ideas, increasing Yield even more. *Forbes* magazine included HCL in its list of Asia's Fab 100 Companies because of its Yield-driven innovation.[15]

Another way to spark innovation is by designing contests. Yield recognizes that many people are motivated by the joy of discovery and attendant reputation for being an innovator. The best contests open the competition to a diverse group of employees, so include the entire company. Use the power of the crowd to improve business processes, and then have a public Ovation for the winner. Innovators come from all walks of life. The top entry in Netflix's contest to improve its recommendation algorithm came from a retired management consultant named Gavin Potter who had a degree in psychology and won using help from his teenaged daughter to get the math right.

To set high eXpectations for contests, use hackathons or innovation jams that run for short periods of time to focus attention and generate ideas rapidly. Cisco's I-Prize was a contest to discover a new billion-dollar business, first run internally and then opened to customers. A German-Russian team won the $250,000 prize for developing smart energy grid software that used Cisco's advantage in information processing.[16] The Yield approach to assessing solutions has colleagues vote rather than using a panel of experts to evaluate them, just like HCL Technologies does. You can use crowdsourcing platforms like Brightidea or BigNerve to facilitate this process.

Rapid reactions. Yield is especially important when an organization's operational environment is volatile. When Gen. Stanley McChrystal commanded U.S. forces in Afghanistan and Iraq, he set up a fast-reaction army unit called TF714. Although the U.S. military traditionally practices top-down control, McChrystal designed TF714 so that midlevel officers and senior noncommissioned officers could rapidly execute fluid plans without senior officer approval. This high-Yield unit captured Saddam Hussein and tracked and killed the leader of Al-Qaeda in Iraq, Abu Musab al-Zarqawi.[17] It was able to do this because war fighters could innovate on the fly.

Yield can awaken the latent skills of colleagues. Hiring for a specific skill set ignores the abilities colleagues may have that can improve productivity. High-Yield companies build flexible processes that can be modified rapidly, like the Lean manufacturing used at the Toyota-GM NUMMI plant. Yield encourages continuous experimentation. Thomas Edison wrote, "I have not failed, I've just found 10,000 ways that won't work."[18]

Yield for all. Yield can be successfully implemented across job categories. In 2003, Cali Ressler and Jody Thompson developed new management guidelines at Best Buy, the large electronics retailer. They called their plan ROWE, for Results-Only Work Environment. A key component of ROWE is a company-wide policy of Yield. Supervisors set clear eXpectations for colleagues, who then chose how, when, and where to do their work. Set work hours were abolished along with a set number of sick days. By clarifying eXpectations and how objectives were measured, team members focused on meeting goals rather than "presenteeism."[19] Best Buy colleagues gained ownership over projects, and those who reached their goals were recognized with Ovation. ROWE treats colleagues as knowledge workers who can determine how best to accomplish their goals. ROWE thrives on broad knowledge sharing so innovations are copied. After ROWE was implemented, voluntary turnover rates fell 90 percent, and productivity increased 41 percent.[20] Yield at Best Buy was scaled back in 2012 when Hubert Joly took over as CEO and faced shrinking profit margins. Joly said that a high-Yield culture did not fit his leadership style in which "direction needs to come from the top."[21] Only time will tell if Joly's changes produce a turnaround for Best Buy, but he is certainly signaling to employees that he does not trust them to manage their work lives themselves.

This leads us to an important point: Yield needs to be embraced by supervisors or it is destined to fail. A trucking company did a randomized controlled experiment of Yield by instructing one-half of managers to allow colleagues to choose maintenance contractors, nighttime road service coverage, and how to handle complaints. The other managers made these decisions and had others implement them as was usual. Four months after the change, the colleagues who were endowed with Yield reported increased commitment to the organization's goals, higher job satisfaction, and reduced accident frequency but with an important caveat: Supervisor support was necessary. When supervisors offered encouragement to those in the Yield group and permitted them to make mistakes, engagement and performance improved. Without it, Yield fell flat.[22]

Barry-Wehmiller has strong leadership support for Yield and has documented the value it creates. Suggestions from colleagues like "Joe" who have deep knowledge of products and processes drive continuous improvements that boost the bottom line. A year after the Wisconsin manufacturing plant was reorganized, products were being delivered on time, output quality had improved, overtime was cut, and new colleagues were being hired. Profits? Stable and growing.

Like Barry-Wehmiller, Whole Foods Markets has embraced Yield from the executive suite to the store aisles. Each department in its stores is run as a nearly autonomous unit, deciding what it will sell, whom to hire, and how to display products. Departments have their own profit-and-loss statements and are responsible for staying in the black. Teams are arranged in a lattice so they can learn from others' successes and mistakes. Bonuses are team based and include everyone. Walter Robb, co-CEO of Whole Foods, has said, "When leaders give their power away to others, they create space for those people to flourish."[23] As we'll see in chapter 11, Robb is right; high-trust organizations are more successful using multiple measures.

☕ MONDAY MORNING LIST

▶ Hold innovation jams to crowdsource ideas, act on them, and recognize those who offer actionable suggestions.

▶ Permit colleagues to set their own work hours in one department and track the effect on productivity.

▶ Empower colleagues by rotating team leadership for each project.

▶ Stimulate innovation by holding a quarterly "Bloopers & Burgers" event where mistakes are celebrated and discussed.

▶ Institutionalize post-project debriefs using "three things right, three things wrong" so all opinions are heard.

Chapter 5

Transfer

Transfer enables self-management by permitting colleagues to craft their own jobs. Transfer explains 82 percent of organizational trust.

Could job titles become obsolete? While individual colleagues have specialized skills, aren't we all working for the same goals? If so, why are titles (and, for that matter, promotions) really necessary? One of the fastest growing and most profitable agricultural companies in the United States, The Morning Star Company has no job titles. Everyone is a colleague. Even owner-founder Chris Rufer's business card has just his name on it. Each colleague chooses which work group to join based on a commitment to create value for the group.[1] Morning Star produces more than half of the U.S. output of processed tomato products (sauce, paste, and stewed tomatoes) and has nearly single-handedly driven down the price of these products by 80 percent over the last 30 years. Rufer attributes the company's success to its culture of excellence and extreme efficiency.[2]

Transfer is Yield on steroids. It allows colleagues the freedom to choose how, when, and where they do their work. Sounds like the rise of the knowledge worker, right? Certainly. But, could it go beyond that?

During half a dozen visits to Morning Star, I have interviewed a cross section of its 2,500 colleagues. These are people who harvest tomatoes, drive trucks, and keep enormous tomato-processing machines running. These men and women define blue collar. Eighty percent of the colleagues at Morning Star are seasonal. They pick, clean, and process tomatoes for four months a year. Year after year they return, asking to join work groups by writing a "Colleague Letter of Understanding" stating how they will create value for their group. Teams of colleagues set schedules, drive efficiency gains, and mediate disputes. They also choose their own career paths. My interviews and data from the Ofactor survey reveal that Morning Star colleagues are highly engaged and really happy. They earn a 30 percent premium over employees at other tomato-processing companies because Morning Star has cut layers of management. This also means that Morning Star can be choosy about whom it hires.

Transfer does not mean colleagues are cut loose to work on their own. During one of my visits, I met a young woman who sorted tomatoes going by on a sluice by color and to remove nontomato material (interestingly, I was told only women can do this job because men get too dizzy). She had slipped and hurt her knee and it had swollen up, so her teammates arranged for her to receive a medical evaluation. We chatted as she waited for a taxi to a nearby urgent care center. I asked about health care, disability insurance to cover lost wages, and if she felt taken care of by the company. She was amazingly upbeat about everything. In fact, I found that two and sometimes three generations in a family worked at Morning Star's plants. Job mobility was fairly easy for those who wanted it, and family education benefits had recently been provided. Processing tomatoes is a highly regulated industry. Each plant has a U.S. Food and Drug Administration lab on-site randomly testing for quality and cleanliness. Excellence is necessary at every stage of the production process, and it is achieved with Transfer.

Transfer barriers. So why don't all organizations institute Transfer? It is starting. Fully one-third of the U.S. workforce is part of the so-called gig economy. These people work for multiple employers simultaneously.[3] At the same time, a survey of more than 36,000 employees in 18 countries reported that only 3 percent of companies have high levels of Transfer.[4] Yet people have a clear desire to control their work lives. A 2012 Intelligent Office Work IQ Survey found that nearly two-thirds of employees aspire to be autonomous at work.[5] This is driven by a desire for freedom, the maintenance of a reasonable work-life integration, and the mobility afforded by technology. Oh, and zero percent reported their goal was to be a corporate executive.

One reason that more companies do not embrace Transfer is that the factors in the OXYTOCIN paradigm that precede Transfer must be in place before self-management is effective: Ovations must celebrate wins and identify the causes of mistakes, eXpectations must be clearly set and supported, and supervisors must effectively Yield control of the execution of projects to others. A recent Gallup survey reported that 81 percent of employees would prefer to manage themselves if their company creates the right culture for it (and 29 percent want to manage themselves now, even in their existing culture). As we'll discuss in this chapter, a culture of Transfer has been successful across a variety of industries, including service companies like DaVita, Zappos, Buurtzorg Nederland, and Precision Nutrition; manufacturers like Semco and W. L. Gore; and tech companies like Menlo Innovations and Valve Software.

Your organization can follow their leads and create of culture of Transfer, too.

Transfer on the brain. By enabling people to control their work lives, Transfer inhibits the production of the hormone cortisol.[6] Cortisol is the body's primary chronic-stress chemical. When raised for extended periods of time, it hardens the arteries, leading to heart attacks. It floods the bloodstream with glucose, leading to diabetes. And it attacks the hippocampus, the brain's key structure for consolidating experiences into learning. Chronically high cortisol is literally a killer.

At the same time, those who lack autonomy at work feel devalued and suffer more depressive moods.[7] The American Psychological Association lists autonomy as one of four components of psychological well-being (the others are relatedness, competence, and self-esteem).[8] Sufficient autonomy is necessary for mental and physical health as well as for full engagement at work.

The desire for autonomy is not just a Western ideal. A study of over 5,000 managers from 24 locations in developing and developed countries confirms that Transfer increases job satisfaction and motivation.[9] It does this because individuals know when they are ready to engage with the day's work tasks and can prioritize them for highest impact. Transfer does not mean working alone. On the contrary, when empowered with Transfer, people have to create or join teams and must be clear about the value they bring to each one. Transfer also builds social connections because self-managing colleagues have to move between teams rapidly.

Job crafting. One way to implement Transfer is through job crafting. Let colleagues design their jobs around what they love doing, rather than assigning them to do tasks. Colleagues can coordinate to do the parts of the whole that they enjoy the most while still covering the functions the organization needs to have done. This feeds people's creativity and enthusiasm and reduces the risk of burnout. By allowing colleagues to craft jobs, and re-craft jobs over time, engagement is sustained. Job crafting can involve stretching oneself to take on tasks that may at first appear difficult to master. Remember from chapter 3 that hard but doable tasks are highly motivating.[10]

Valve Corporation is a quintessential high-Transfer organization. Valve develops online games like Counter-Strike, Half-Life, Portal, and Left 4 Dead. Valve employees are not assigned to a work group; rather, they are given desks with wheels. They are then encouraged to shop around and see what projects others are working on and join a project that seems "interesting" and "rewarding.[11] The comic-book-like and extremely short employee handbook states in a section called "What if I Screw Up?" that "Providing the freedom to fail is an important trait of [Valve]—we couldn't expect so much of individuals if we also penalized people for errors. Even expensive mistakes, or ones which result in a very public failure, are genuinely looked at as opportunities to learn."[12] No work is assigned to colleagues in this flat organization, there are no bosses, and colleagues rotate being the lead on projects. Valve does not even have traditional sales or marketing departments, expecting customers to find them through word of mouth.[13] Work groups evaluate peer contributions after every project ends (debrief) and practice Ovation constantly. This is Transfer at its best. Valve has grown to over 300 colleagues, and its market value is estimated to be $2.5 billion.

Companies like Valve that practice Transfer have few layers of management between line workers and the C-suite. Nucor, a large, second-generation steel producer based in Charlotte, North Carolina, is another flat organization. Nucor has grown from $21 million in revenue in 1966 to over $20 billion today. The company attributes its success to a decentralized culture, the freedom to try new things and fail, and egalitarian compensation.[14] Nucor has only four management levels separating employees from the CEO and just 90 employees working in the executive office. Transfer is practiced at Nucor by trusting most operational decisions to division managers. Former CEO Dan DiMicco has said Nucor's management philosophy is, "Hire the right people, give them the resources and tools, and get the hell out of the way."[15]

Adults at work. Selecting the right colleagues is important when designing a high-Transfer workplace because colleagues have to figure out how to cooperate with each other and hold each other accountable.[16] Some people are unwilling or uninterested in managing themselves. A colleague I spoke to at Morning Star who drove a harvesting machine said he disliked self-management because it made him "think too much." When Zappos.com implemented a company-wide Transfer program in 2015, colleagues were invited to quit and take three months' severance if they were not fully committed to self-management. Fourteen percent did so.[17] By setting eXpectations clearly, those for whom a culture of Transfer is not a good fit can be identified and trained or offered a buyout.

Sometimes the easiest way to institute transfer is by disappearing. Patagonia Inc., a Ventura, California, maker of outdoor gear for "dirtbags" who thrive by climbing, paddling, and hiking, has a lunchtime surfing group. Colleagues are accountable for completing their projects (eXpectation), but if the surf is up at noon and people would prefer to finish their work at night, why should anyone care? Founder Yvon Chouinard regularly disappears for months at a time to explore the world. Chouinard calls this Management By Absence (MBA). Transfer is even used at Patagonia's retail stores, where colleagues are cross-trained and schedule themselves to cover store hours. A store manager told me that if an employee says, "Let me get my manager," the customer has the impression that training and responsibility are lacking. Patagonia has found that most decisions can be made by store associates without a manager's oversight. Patagonia has been described as "a company that profits as it pampers workers."[18]

What's so special about working 8 to 5 anyway? This is just a social convention that does not fit the lifestyle of many volunteer-employees. Just as Taylorism failed when it sought to break tasks into small bits that could be done without thinking, the standard workday is a form of micromanagement that does not suit many valuable colleagues. If there is work to be done, why not let colleagues choose what to do and when to do it?

Ricardo Semler, CEO of Brazilian manufacturing company Semco, calls Transfer "treating employees like adults." Semco is a fully democratic company in which decisions are made on a one-person, one-vote basis, with Semler receiving only a single vote. Colleagues are responsible for managing their time and meeting with team members to complete projects. At Semco, all meetings are optional. eXpectations are clearly set, and colleagues must demonstrate the value they create for the organization to continue working there.[19] Alexis de Tocqueville argued in *Democracy in America* (1835) that an all-powerful government infantilizes its citizens. An all-powerful organizational leadership does the same thing to colleagues. People manage to wake up on time, get dressed, and get to work, so why do we micromanage them when they get to work?

Rules versus discretion. Treating colleagues like adults means giving them discretion rather than shackling them with rules—even if they are Lutherans. Lutherans embrace their German heritage and are comfortable following rules. But when Bill McKinney joined Thrivent Financial for Lutherans (now Thrivent Financial) as a vice president in 2003, the rules were out of control at the 100-year-old, $8 billion, Fortune 500 company.

Thrivent had exquisitely detailed rules about how much one could spend on meals during travel, including when an alcoholic drink would be reimbursed and when it would not; when one could buy a client a meal and when one could not; and a long, detailed dress code. Employees spent a huge amount of time documenting their compliance with these rules. To combat rule creep, McKinney and colleagues formed a "rule-busting committee." The committee would identify rules that burned employee time and suggest policies that substituted judgment for blind rule following. They started with travel. Travel expenses would only be reviewed quarterly, and reasonable expenses did not have to be justified. The dress code was replaced with the advice to "dress for the job you want."

Thrivent's rule-busting committee has replaced dozens of rules with good judgment, empowering employees to act like owners and consider the costs and benefits of their choices. Thrivent's return on investment continues to beat its rivals', and its colleagues have a stake in its performance with generous profit-sharing programs.[20]

Google's take on reducing rules is called "bureaucracy busters." In a very Googley approach, colleagues vote on which rules to eliminate. This list is then implemented by department directors. In some years, departments have eliminated 20 rules. This is a simple way to reduce the frustration that gets in the way of doing excellent work. A favorite busted rule at Google was getting rid of the submission of paper receipts for travel expenses. Now Googlers take a photo of the receipt with their phones and email it for reimbursement.

Airbnb, the accommodations-rental company, calls this approach "replacing policy with principles." Or, more simply, using a "gut check," according to Mike Curtis, vice president of engineering. At Airbnb expenses under $500 do not need approval. If colleagues want to spend more than $500, they are asked to think about whether the purchase is really needed. Colleagues are trusted to use good judgment. Airbnb did not see an increase in discretionary spending after this policy change and saved lots of time by eliminating paperwork.[21] Morning Star similarly permits colleagues to purchase needed supplies or equipment by spending up to $10,000 without approval—as long as they consult with their colleagues first.[22]

Transferring commitment. A meta-analysis of 114 studies of Transfer involving over 20,000 participants in laboratory and field experiments found that a 5 percent increase in empowerment (a proxy for Transfer) powerfully stoked performance, raising it by 28 percent.[23] A related study of employees at work showed that an increase in Transfer raised productivity, customer service, job satisfaction, and organizational commitment.[24]

Transfer even works for often underpaid and often underappreciated government employees. A management experiment taught civil servants about self-management, handling job and family stresses, and goal setting. It also asked colleagues to write a set of self-administered rewards and punishments for meeting or missing goals. This program resulted in a 6 percent increase in hours worked among frequently absent unionized state employees. The effect continued and even improved 12 months after the intervention, increasing hours worked by 15 percent from preintervention levels.[25]

Sometimes Transfer comes about because there is no other option. In the 1990s, the fast-food chain Taco Bell was rapidly expanding. But it had a shortage of managers and did not want to simply hire warm bodies to fill open positions. It solved this problem using a two-pronged approach. The first prong was to create a small number of regional managers who were well trained and well paid. The second prong was to endow its thousands of line workers with Transfer. Regional managers invested the time to train entry-level cooks, cashiers, and cleaning staff to manage themselves. Minimum-wage employees were trained to hire and train new employees, manage inventory, account for cash in and out of the store, and maintain communication with regional managers. Taco Bell's analyses found that colleagues were highly engaged and created valuable innovations that were often spread company-wide. For example, during slow hours, Taco Bell colleagues started their own cross-training program, doing different jobs than those to which they were assigned in order to advance in the company. The freedom of Transfer also boosted customer satisfaction ratings and store profits.[26]

The Dutch home-patient-care company Buurtzorg Nederland produced similar outcomes when it put nurses in charge. They call this the "primary nursing model." Nurses have the most information about what their patients need, so Buurtzorg asked nurses to organize themselves into teams to coordinate all aspects of care. This is effective for several reasons. Teams are kept small, with no more than 12 nurses, easing coordination. Senior nurse-coaches assist up to 45 nurse teams to answer questions and ensure compliance with regulations. Buurtzorg also developed software to share information across teams and develop a catalog of best practices. Ninety-one percent of clients are satisfied with Buurtzorg's care, while employee satisfaction is at the 89th percentile.[27] Academic analyses show that Buurtzorg is 43 percent more efficient than other nursing firms in the Netherlands, and its patients end up in the emergency department substantially less. Buurtzorg's motto is, "How do you manage professionals? You don't!"[28]

Transfer in teams. Transfer effectively engages colleagues by building reliance on team members: "*We* need to accomplish this goal if *I* am going to be successful." Once eXpectations are set, if one or more colleagues drop the ball, the team suffers. This motivates teams to manage themselves and remediate or remove underperformers. Transfer promotes the nimbleness necessary to be successful.

You can start a program of Transfer by asking colleagues to volunteer to lead a project rather than assigning it to someone. This not only demonstrates trust, it uses individuals' information about their own capacity and ability to complete projects. Even the language you use can reinforce Transfer. Titles like *volunteer, colleague,* and *teammate* are a good start.

Captain David Marquet, former commander of the nuclear-powered submarine USS *Santa Fe,* nudged his team toward Transfer by changing the language used on his ship. In the hierarchical model of command, officers would request permission to do something, like submerge the ship. Then the commanding officer would reply, "Submerge the ship," confirming the request. Marquet instructed his officers to use the word *intend* instead of *request,* informing others of the officer's actions but not asking permission. The officer at the helm might say, "Captain, I intend to the submerge the ship." The captain would then acknowledge the intention, and the helmsman would do the job without being micromanaged. The captain can still countermand the intention, but the language says to the crew, "You are in charge." Marquet has proposed that as an organization increases in Transfer, the language used changes from asking for permission to phrases like "I intend," "I just did," and then to "I have been doing."[29]

Transfer is starting to infiltrate the U.S. Navy more broadly. In 2015, I worked with the navy's Strategic Studies Group as it developed a program to transform how the navy selects, evaluates, promotes, and retains sailors in the 21st century. Lt. Cdr. Michael Tsonis and his colleagues have identified two key factors that they need to change in the rigid command-and-control structure of the navy to improve the performance of sailors: Transfer and trust. They understand that decision-making power needs to be devolved to small units of sailors to obtain full commitment to outcomes and to create an engaging career path. The process they are developing is focused on increasing Transfer while ensuring that sailors stay safe and are effective warriors.[30]

You are your brand. Often, the most stressful part of an employee's job is interacting with a supervisor.[31] A shocking 97 percent of 36,000 employees surveyed reported that their supervisors are coercive, autocratic, or highly controlling.[32] Transfer promotes emotional stability by reducing the stress of reporting to the boss. In high-Transfer organizations, you are your own boss. Peter Drucker wrote, "The modern organization cannot be thought of as an organization of bosses and subordinates. It must be organized as a team of associates."[33] If you are the boss, start treating others as equals. At preeminent U.S. metals producer Alcoa, a modicum of Transfer was enabled by eliminating executive parking places. Colleagues who arrived early got the best parking spots.[34] We will discuss what leaders can do to increase trust in chapter 9, but if you want to lead a high-Transfer organization, you need to give up control and empower others.

There is a middle ground between hierarchical control and complete self-management. London management consulting company Eden McCallum thinks it has found that space. It has a pool of 500 consultants who work for it, but none are on the payroll. They work on what they want, when they want. Eden McCallum found it could hire talented senior consultants who had been partners at McKinsey or Bain but dreaded the administrative work and meetings they were required to attend. When Eden McCallum has a project to do, it alerts its specialists and asks who is interested in the project. Overhead is kept low, as a small group of partners manage administrative duties and secure new business.[35] This model provides Eden McCallum with a large set of experienced consultants who can complete work less expensively than can companies that have bloated administrations and pay partners handsomely. In essence, Eden McCallum runs a spot market that matches the demand for consulting services with the supply of consultants. It is the flexibility that Transfer enables that makes Eden McCallum successful.

A culture of flexibility is a good indicator of a high-Transfer organization. Sixty-four percent of LinkedIn members said they would value more flexibility at work over a 10 percent pay raise.[36] Organizations high in Transfer have flexible work hours and shared work spaces, encourage remote work and the use of coworking spaces, and use technology to reduce travel. Various studies have shown that telecommuters are more productive than in-office colleagues. Much of this gain is due to the reduced time and stress of commuting. Those who work from home report greater job satisfaction and quit their jobs at lower rates than traditional employees.[37] While 63 percent of companies allow telecommuting, only one-third of supervisors say they trust their colleagues to work without supervision. That's the Transfer disconnect.[38] A German study found that when colleagues set their own work schedules, they put in 7.4 more hours a week than required.[39] Letting colleagues figure how to meet expectations themselves is highly engaging.

Winning the war on talent. Tech companies have been the fastest to respond to the demand for flexibility because the pool of talented colleagues is so limited. Enterprise software company InDinero created a Transfer culture it calls entre-ocracy. InDinero maintains the flat organizational structure and autonomy it had as a start-up by refusing to hire middle managers and making decisions collaboratively. This gives all employees a voice and uses the wisdom of the crowd to improve outcomes. It does this even for salaries and bonuses.[40] Transfer works at InDinero in part because it scrupulously quantifies colleague performance and shares this information throughout the company (more on why this is important in chapter 6). Transfer flourishes with objective and continuous measurement of goals.

In the early 2000s, Blue Cross Blue Shield of Massachusetts noticed it was losing high-performing colleagues to competitors who permitted telecommuting. In a well-designed management experiment, it tested the effect of working from home by letting 150 colleagues try it. It was a success: Work was completed and colleagues were happier. Currently, over 700 Blue Cross Blue Shield of Massachusetts colleagues, about 20 percent of its staff, work full-time outside the office. Not only has this aided retention, but the company has been able to trim office space, saving $8.5 million a year on leasing costs. It is currently testing "hot desking," in which colleagues reserve a desk for days they want to work in the office and leave it for others when they work from afar. Not only does this further reduce office space requirements, it also lets those from different teams get to know each other while they share space.[41]

Another company that thrives on Transfer is the high-end office designer Herman Miller. Its Holland Michigan Design Yard has gorgeous open-office designs, spaces for individual work, glass-walled meeting rooms, and has wireless throughout. My lab ran a neuroscience experiment at Herman Miller to quantify the effect that space configurations have on colleague collaboration. We obtained neurologic and behavioral data from 96 employees working in three open-office configurations. We found that those working in the most-open office space had significantly more focus on tasks, innovated more when working in groups, and shed the challenge stress of work more rapidly than those who worked in more-closed spaces. Colleagues in the most-open location were also happier, felt closer to their colleagues, and had more trust in them compared with those working in less-open spaces. Our findings suggest that an open-office plan can enhance Transfer and improve collaboration.[42]

During a visit to the preeminent design group IDEO, I asked CEO Tim Brown why he had remained at the company so long. He said it was "because I redesign my position every five years." At IDEO, even the CEO gets Transfer.[43]

Banishing time clocks. Netflix, Best Buy, HubSpot, Automattic, Twitter, Zygna, and Virgin Group have recently adopted another aspect of Transfer: They have stopped counting workdays. Do you need the afternoon off? Take it. Want to relax for two weeks in Capri? Sure. As long as your team is working on its projects, and eXpectations are being fulfilled, where, when, and how one does one's work is not relevant. The increase in trust is supplemented by the reduction in paperwork and accounting costs. In 2015, Netflix went further: It offered new parents 16 weeks of paid leave and unlimited unpaid leave in the first year after their child is born. Netflix had already established a strong Transfer culture, so this parental leave policy fits in well. That is important: Giving more freedom to colleagues makes sense in a culture that has already embraced Transfer. Reed Hastings, founder and CEO of Netflix, echoes Ricardo Semler in saying his company's culture treats employees "like fully-formed adults," and he attributes Netflix's success to its high level of Transfer.[44]

Of course, not accounting for hours at work could lead to overwork. As we discussed in chapter 3, overworking colleagues drives them out of your organization. At the same time, self-managed colleagues understand that if they do not contribute sufficiently to the organization's goals, their employment will not continue. One way to resolve this conflict is how Valve software and my lab do it: Rotate the project lead around so the extra burden of leadership is shared and everyone learns to lead a team. Team leaders tend to work longer hours since they are ultimately responsible for the success of a project. Andrew Kay, founder of pioneering PC maker Kaypro, developed a great way to implement Transfer: "We regard management as basically an affair of teaching and training, not one of directing and controlling. We control the process, not the people."[45]

Another solution to potential overwork is to emphasize the importance of taking vacations. A global survey found that colleagues who take more vacation time work more efficiently when they are on the job. With only 10 vacation days, the typical full-time U.S. colleague lags well behind the time taken by those in most other developed countries (and only 25 percent of Americans use all of their vacation time).[46] But there is pushback: 2 percent of companies have unlimited paid vacations, and this trend is growing according to a 2015 survey by the Society for Human Resource Management. Volunteer-employees empowered with Transfer can choose when and how much vacation to take. And this means everyone. Top executives need to set the example by disappearing for a while and letting others run the show.

Yvon Chouinard, founder of Patagonia, has described his management philosophy as, "Let my people go (surfing)."[47] Companies like Patagonia that create a culture of Transfer untether and empower colleagues.

Transfer works best in an environment of Openness. The next chapter explains why.

☕ MONDAY MORNING LIST

▸ Create a democratic workplace by having colleagues vote on Start, Stop, or Continue when reviewing projects, and act on the vote.

▸ Ask team members to complete an annual Colleague Letter of Understanding in which they write down how they create value for the organization.

▸ Reduce hierarchy by eliminating or reducing job titles by using *colleague, associate,* or *team member* to identify people.

▸ Scrap the vacation policy; let people manage their own time.

▸ Start a rule-busting committee and act on its recommendations.

Chapter 6

Openness

Openness shares information broadly with colleagues. Openness explains 65 percent of organizational trust.

Salaries? Posted online. Revenue and number of customers? Ditto. Company emails? Accessible by everyone. Openness about personal goals? Sure, trackable by your colleagues using idoneThis software so everyone can see if you're living a rich, happy life.

Radical Openness? That's certainly a term for it.

Openness is part of the core business model at Buffer, a software company that optimizes social media impact. "Transparency breeds trust, and trust is the foundation of great teamwork." That's not me saying this, it is Buffer founder and CEO Joel Gascoigne.[1] Within three years of its 2010 founding, Buffer was serving 1 million customers a day.

Sure, you're thinking, another wacky, Burning Man-attending software engineer who thinks he can start a successful company.

But the science backs up Buffer's focus on Openness as a way to bolster trust.

As we learned in chapter 3, chronic stress is a trust buster. The two consistent sources of stress are one's boss (solutions for that were in chapter 5) and not knowing the boss's plans. Where is this company going? Why are we acquiring XYZ Corp.? Will we be sold? Are layoffs coming? These types of questions are on the minds of colleagues daily. They are chronic stressors that can be dissipated by Openness. This chapter shows you how to create a culture of Openness.

Only 40 percent of employees report that they are well informed about their company's goals, strategies, and tactics.[2] Yet copious evidence shows that when an organization's colleagues know why decisions are being made, they are more motivated and productive. You cannot expect colleagues to behave like owners unless they know the organization's heading and destination. Just like a pilot files a flight plan before takeoff, executives who share the organization's flight plan with colleagues reduce uncertainty about the journey. While Yield opens the flow of information from colleagues on the front lines to supervisors, its reciprocal, Openness, asks supervisors to share information broadly with colleagues. This two-way street builds trust.

Dialysis and kidney-care company DaVita practices Openness by encouraging open communication among team members in their daily homeroom meetings and monthly town hall meetings. DaVita CEO Kent Thiry holds regular phone conferences in which any "teammate" (not employee) can ask him a question and get an immediate answer that all can hear. Openness works at DaVita because it has thoughtfully built a culture of sharing. DaVita "villages" are groups of treatment centers that define their own identities and provide open communication with other villages. Each village is run as independent businesses (Transfer) where every teammate has a say in decisions. Bureaucracy is actively minimized by sharing information broadly. This allows for rapid responses to local markets (Yield) and reinforces inclusivity. Teammates get regular profit-sharing payouts based on locally chosen success metrics. DaVita's open culture has worked: It generates $8 billion in annual revenue.

Organizations high on Openness tend to have flat management structures and simple lines of communication. Openness does not require self-management like The Morning Star Company or Semco, but reduced hierarchy aids Openness. Google's Project Oxygen tested if a reduction in hierarchy affected productivity. In fact, it asked if managers matter at all. It found that they did, especially in setting eXpectations, being Caring (chapter 7), and facilitating Openness. Based on those findings and some experimentation with self-management, Google settled on a management structure that keeps hierarchy to the bare minimum.[3] Google discovered that Googlers have more motivation when leaders share a great deal of information. This was especially true when it came to information on strategic directions that the company was taking and the rationale for decisions. Google has not eliminated managers, but it sees them more as coaches and communication conduits than as czars.[4]

A 2015 study of 2.5 million manager-led teams in 195 countries by the Gallup organization confirmed Google's findings. It found that workforce engagement improved when supervisors had some form of daily communication with direct reports.[5] A team is more effective when people know where they are headed and why.

Inclusive listening. Even the U.S. Air Force is replacing the us-versus-them mentality with Openness. The hazing of new cadets at the Air Force Academy, with the tacit approval of the leadership, was undermining authority and diminishing morale. The "because I say so" leadership style caused cadets to dislike leaders and led to frequent infractions of the exhaustive conduct rules. To fix these problems, the academy leadership first set clear eXpectations for cadets. It then set them for leaders. This was done with Openness about the problems cadets and leaders faced. One source of infractions was pervasive alcohol abuse. This was reduced by scaling back required weekend activities so cadets could socialize and build friendships like other college students. Another Openness innovation was including junior officers and cadets in discussions about academy policies. Maj. Gen. Gregory Lengyel, former commandant of cadets at the academy, has said, "I'm not—by far—the smartest guy on my team." By opening communication, Lengyel allowed cadets to take ownership of decisions. Openness caused morale to soar and infractions to fall.[6]

Even without an explicit intervention, leaders can evaluate the effects of naturally occurring differences on Openness to find out what works. An examination of the variation in Openness by clinical nurse managers in a hospital found that managers who shared more information were more trusted by colleagues, and their units performed better. Managers who shared the "why" behind eXpectations with nurses tapped into the intrinsic motivation to perform well for one's teammates. This natural experiment shows how one can find an improvement in one department that can be implemented throughout the organization.

Inclusion and diversity are powerful Openness levers. More and different opinions improve decisions and can provide fresh insights. By one estimate, women and minorities were responsible for 15 to 20 percent of U.S. economic growth from 1960 to 2008.[7] Their opinions matter. Include everyone's opinions when creating a culture of Openness. By listening to and sharing information with everyone, you can create a fair and democratic workplace. Otherwise, why would everyone be equally engaged at work?

Open salaries. You do not have to plunge your organization headfirst into radical Openness like at Buffer. Even modest steps to increase Openness can improve productivity. A study by Emiliano Huet-Vaughn of Middlebury College randomly informed one-half of employees doing piece-rate work about the pay of their colleagues. The other half remained in the dark about others' pay. Those in the Openness condition were 10 percent more productive when assessed weeks later than those in the control group.[8]

Making salaries public helps ensure fairness and prompts discussions of what people are doing that merit differences in pay. My lab constantly writes proposals to fund our research, and many people help prepare them. I presume that when a budget shows I will spend a month of my time on a project, my colleagues can multiply by 12 and determine my annual salary. In order to embrace Openness, I decided to meet with my team and discuss salaries (which are set by my university). Why do I make more than they do as a professor and lab director? I outlined the mostly hidden tasks that I do that help support their work and make us successful, including a seemingly endless number of meetings and near-constant travel that takes me away from my family. Having my colleagues understand what I do every day made me feel great. Others then began discussing what they do that team members do not see. I discovered that no one really cared about salary differences. People were more interested in doing important and challenging work, and we gained an understanding of how each person's contribution made this possible.

Open doors. Of course, one has to be careful when creating a culture of Openness. Some things should be kept private, like client information or research and development data. This starts with office space. As discussed in chapter 5, my lab ran an experiment showing that people working in open office plans are more productive and innovative than those working in a cube farm. But most colleagues still want to have a place to store their stuff, put up a few photos, and tuck away their purse or backpack. Balancing shared work spaces that facilitate communication with half-height nooks, glass-walled conference rooms, and quiet work areas are reasonable compromises that can accommodate Openness and offer some privacy.

Jerre Stead, CEO of several Fortune 100 technology companies, told me how he instituted an Openness policy when he took the helm at business machine manufacturer NCR Corp. in 1993. First, he moved his office from the penthouse suite, where a security guard blocked access to the executive elevator, to an open space with other executives. Everyone knew that if you wanted to find Jerre, he would be in the pit with everyone else. Next, he started a monthly get-together for 25 colleagues at a time called "Juice with Jerre." Any employee could sign up to have juice and air complaints, ask questions, or just find out where the company was going. Stead would take the time to explain why things were being done so people understood his turnaround strategy.

Stead also instituted an open-door policy for all offices. He believed that Openness could not infiltrate NCR if information was kept behind closed doors. Still, some doors have to stay closed, for example, in human resources or some offices in accounting and finance, but Stead wanted almost all doors to be open. That privacy crack in the open-door policy led, some months later, to many closed doors. So, one Sunday, Stead had the facilities crew meet him at the office, and he asked them to remove *every* interior door. You might say this was a prank, but he sent a clear message that NCR was embracing Openness. Items that had to be kept private were put into locked filing cabinets, but the doors were history.[9]

Openness can start internally and grow to be shared externally. HubSpot is a Boston-based marketing software company that posts financial data, board meeting decks, strategy memos, and sometimes funny internal documents on its website. CEO and founder Brian Halligan has said, "Culture is to recruiting as product is to marketing." HubSpot created a "Culture Code" that specifies what its culture entails and how the company knows if it is being true to it. One of its tenets is radical Openness. Nearly every piece of information is shared with all 800 employees. Exceptions to this rule, stated in the Culture Code, include not sharing when the company cannot legally do so (when a nondisclosure statement was signed), and not sharing compensation data when an individual can be identified.[10]

Privacy and Openness. Yield is another balancing factor for Openness. Sometimes privacy can encourage people to try something new, even in a culture that discourages changes. Ethan Bernstein at Harvard Business School had a moveable curtain put around several production lines at a Chinese mobile-phone factory to test the effect of privacy. Productivity rose 10 to 15 percent compared to production lines without curtains. Bernstein found that privacy allowed Chinese workers a modicum of Yield, so they experimented with different approaches to fixing production problems.[11] One way to apply this to your company is to establish a skunkworks where people noodle with the craziest of ideas. The innovations that end up being useful can be shared with others once the kinks are ironed out.

Some of the most sensitive documents in an organization outline strategies and key objectives. Distributing these throughout the organization is an effective way to create Openness. Google is a leader in sharing its key objectives so every team knows where the company is going. This information lets teams adjust their own strategies if they are out of alignment with the company as a whole.[12] Transparent information flows focus colleagues on hitting eXpectations.

What about sharing performance evaluations? At some level, most people know how hard others are working. But full sharing of colleagues' performance evaluations could also result in shame or ostracism. Remember from chapter 2 that one should praise in public but critique in private. Useful comparisons can be done by sharing average colleague performance broadly but individual performance privately. In this way, individuals know if they are above or below average performance, and they and their supervisors can adjust their work flow and training accordingly.

Inverted pyramid. When the performance of each department is shared, then it is clear how well human resources, finance, and administration serve the colleagues who produce the goods and services the organization sells. In this way, Openness can invert the typical organizational pyramid. This puts all colleagues on the same page when seeking to hit company-wide performance goals and breaks down departmental barriers. Openness helps coordinate organizational goals as a team.

Vineet Nayar implemented an Openness upgrade when he became president of HCL Technologies in 2005. At the time, HCL was a second-tier Indian IT provider with high employee attrition and a disappearing margin selling hardware and software. Nayar announced a culture change called "Employee First, Customer Second" at the company's 2006 annual meeting. One of the first changes was to track the effectiveness of each department's service to employees. A Smart Service Desk was designed in which colleagues submitted an electronic ticket for help from an administrative department. Resolution times were tracked, and the status of the ticket could be seen by all. This Openness increased efficiency and demonstrated the leadership's commitment to serving front-line colleagues. Managers were also held accountable to their direct-report colleagues. All managers receive 360-degree feedback that is used for a single purpose: to improve performance. Nayar made it clear that 360s would not affect salaries. This tight feedback loop, as we discussed in chapter 3, permits the brain to instantiate outcomes with rewards, sustaining habit change for high performance.

In another Openness innovation, Nayar and senior leadership began producing an annual video explaining the next year's strategies and sharing it with colleagues. They would then spend several weeks traveling to HCL's offices in India and in some of the 35 countries in which it operates, holding town hall meetings to answer questions about the new strategic plan. These meetings are voluntary, yet turnout hit 75 percent at many locations (this is near-maximum attendance due to travel). Nayar even started sharing his and the senior leadership's 360s publicly so others could see how well they were doing and what they needed to work on.[13] Senior leaders at Google and at the global management consulting firm McKinsey & Co. similarly share their 360s, demonstrating the importance of everyone hitting performance goals. HCL is now a top-tier global IT business generating over $6 billion in revenue per year.

Openness is best practiced in person. Email has a strong gravitational pull, but try to resist it when sharing important information. My lab has run neuroscience experiments showing that neural engagement is higher for in-person interactions than for text or video messages. When we meet others in person, we unconsciously perceive body language, facial expressions, and even odors that give us valuable information over and above the words being spoken. Turn off your phone and give the other person your full attention to maximize your impact on them. Openness thrives on one-on-one meetings. When you see someone in person, you are also investing in building a relationship with that person (more on this in chapter 7). Even if the information is painful, it is best to share it face-to-face.

Reducing uncertainty. The chronic stress that comes from the uncertainty about what will happen in an organization affects parts of the brain that undermine motivation and cognition. Uncertainty causes us to be hyperaware of possible threats: We need to pay attention to everything because danger could arise anywhere. This steals neural bandwidth from the rest of the brain, reducing concentration and productivity. We also lose the ability to properly evaluate future events and to integrate multiple streams of information. Uncertainty puts the brain and body on high alert, wanting to escape from lions and their corporate cousins, pink slips. In a true neurologic sense, you can't think when you face high uncertainty. And you certainly cannot be an effective team member.

Openness reduces the stress of uncertainty by giving people a sense of direction. Our brains are pattern-seeking organs. If there is no pattern, we cannot make sense of our world and we are ruled by stress. Knowing where the organization is going is vitally important. If you also share why the organization is heading where it is, then colleagues are able to build a model of likely outcomes. This reduces cognitive load and enables them to execute more effectively. Even if the future is not rosy, at least you know what is coming and are prepared for it.

When colleagues know where the company is going, they can share this information broadly. For example, companies high on Openness often permit their colleagues to talk about what they do in social media. While rules about sharing need to be in place, Tweeting, posting to Facebook, or Instagramming goings-on at work are great ways to demonstrate Openness internally and externally. In the mid-2000s, Jonathan Schwartz, the CEO of Sun Microsystems, began blogging about Sun's business decisions and even announced his resignation when Oracle bought Sun in a haiku on Twitter. Southwest Airlines started an "online watercooler," a blog called "Nuts About Southwest," where employees post entries about their jobs and personal lives. Zappos employees Tweet on the company's site while at work. Even engineers at Microsoft, a company famous for top-down control, now post uncensored videos and blogs about their projects. With the rise of social media and innumerable website hacks, nothing is private anymore, so why even try. Google is not a search engine; it is a reputation-management system.[14] Openness lets the sun shine on what everyone is doing and thereby removes the occasion to cheat or steal or sin.

When Openness is extended to customers, including discussions of strategy, new product ideas, and feature usability, it can build powerful connections to the company. This approach creates "raving fans" who proselytize for the company and its products. Companies that twist or filter information to put the organization in the best light often get significant blowback when the truth comes out—and it always comes out. If you start with honesty, it is difficult to get into trouble.

Default to Openness. The survey company Qualtrics practices radical Openness to keep engagement and collaboration high. Qualtrics CEO Ryan Smith said, "We're hiring people to think. To do so requires that colleagues have information about the company's direction and goals."[15] Sharing reports, memos, and information about projects lets all of its 1,000-plus employees know what others are doing. It frees them from having to ferret out this information at the watercooler. Qualtrics also practices regular Ovations as a way to recognize the highest performers and build in eXpectations for others. Smith believes that information sharing, along with Ovation, keeps the highest performers from leaving the company.[16]

When in doubt, default to Openness because it saves time and energy compared to hiding information. Yes, this seems counter to the perceived wisdom. But when the books are open to everyone, then the reasons for decisions are clear and surprises can be avoided. Companies like Whole Foods and Trader Joe's share quarterly profit and loss statements with colleagues and pay for classes so that everyone understands them. This facilitates honest information flow from supervisors to colleagues about value creation irrespective of job title. And it focuses everyone on hitting performance goals.

Whole Foods shares information on store operations to motivate colleagues to reach targets, reduce costs, and prepare for a move if a store is unprofitable according to founder and co-CEO John Mackey.[17] Departments at Whole Foods are run like independent ventures as teams source local foods, hire colleagues, and rotate promotional items (Transfer). This cannot work if department leaders are not given the Openness to view store costs and revenues as well as information on the processes used by other store units. Openness informs the reasons behind eXpectations and reinforces why Ovations occur. Otherwise, colleagues subsist on rumors and fear.

Creating owners. Semco, discussed in chapter 5 as a high-Transfer organization, is also high on Openness. Semco shares salary and productivity data throughout the company. If one wants to continue in a work group, the 8 to 12 people with whom one has worked must want you to remain based on your performance and how much you will cost the group. "Counselors" solicit colleagues' opinions on projects before taking a vote on whether to move forward. Founder Ricardo Semler believes that employees need a lot of information to manage themselves and contribute value to the organization.[18]

The Morning Star Company similarly provides rich and widely available information using LCD monitors that show real-time data from sensors that track everything from trucks entering the plants to the percentage of red versus green tomatoes in a truckload to the rate tomatoes are processed. Work groups have goals that are shared throughout the company. Visiting its plants, I was fascinated watching the monitors that showed second by second where the entire operation stood. Slacking off? This is rare since the entire plant would see it. This rich information flow motivates colleagues to make decisions like owners.

Building a culture of Openness can also be done in the public sector. Chris Liu, who became director of Washington State Department of Enterprise Services in 2013, did a culture reboot with a focus on Openness. Liu got rid of his office so he would spend his time working with teams, set clear eXpectations for colleagues, and provided them with constant feedback from mentors. He also purchased software so work flows were internally transparent and trackable for speed and quality. Then Liu shared work-flow processes with the public by posting them online for greater accountability by his staff. This eye-on-the-prize approach was kept on track by having over 100 working groups use daily huddles. Liu also arranged for monthly town hall meetings with state Governor Jay Inslee. Supervisors got out of their desks to acquire and share information with their colleagues, rapidly resolving problems. The result? The average number of process steps was reduced from 93 to 63, requests that had to be redone fell by 35 percent, and monthly productivity increased 61 percent.[19]

Openness steps. Here's how you can implement Openness in your organization. First, leaders need to share information broadly. This can be done in weekly meetings that set eXpectations, but these meetings should also discuss why goals are being set. Second, reinforce Openness with daily huddles for small groups (maximum 15 people, but 5 to 7 is better). This provides an opportunity to share information that is of acute interest. Third, like Jerre Stead, leaders need to be available for questions from all comers at regular times. You could call your meeting "Chocolate with Charlie" or "Tea with Tara" to signal that it is informal and open. In my own "Cookies with the Chair" meetings, I have learned extraordinary things about people with whom I had little contact. The individuals I met, the organization, and I were all better for this modest time investment.

Next, consider making processes and documents open for review. Like Whole Foods, this may require training colleagues how to understand accounting data. But when you inform team members, they start thinking about how their choices affect key objectives. Do you have a salary formula? Specifying one, like Buffer does, provides absolute clarity on a major stressor for employees. If you do not want to go whole hog to fully specify how salaries are determined, you can release information on how many people are in salary bands. This balances Openness with privacy. Once documents are out of the board room, consider posting them online for customers (and competitors) to read. If you are proud of what you are doing and have a profitable business, then sharing the whats and whys of your strategy commit you to them and will not benefit rivals.

☕ MONDAY MORNING LIST

▸ Release quarterly balance sheets to colleagues and be sure they know how to read them.

▸ Hold regular town hall meetings to share objectives and key results.

▸ Buy or create software that shows work being done in real time across the company.

▸ Share executive meeting notes and include a summary explaining why decisions were made.

▸ Create and share salary and bonus formulae.

Chapter 7

Caring

Caring is intentionally building relationships with colleagues. Caring explains 84 percent of organizational trust.

"American business is ruining America." This is what Bob Chapman, chief executive of Barry-Wehmiller Companies, told me when I visited its corporate headquarters in St. Louis.[1] In viewing employees as "human resources," most businesses treat people like replaceable machines rather than as human beings. Chapman took the helm of Barry-Wehmiller in 1975 when it was a small and nearly bankrupt concern after the unexpected death of his father. Today, Barry-Wehmiller has operations on five continents, employs 11,000 people, and generates more than $2.4 billion in annual revenue. This economic success grew from Chapman's focus on people. The company's mission statement is, "Building great people is our business." It does this by establishing a Caring culture at every company it acquires. "When people thrive, companies thrive," Chapman has said.[2]

When Barry-Wehmiller purchased the failing Paper Converting Machine Company in Green Bay, Wisconsin, the plant was shut down for several weeks to reorganize and so that the new managers could engage with the company's colleagues. During one of these sessions, a skeptical union employee said, "I want to hear you say that you care about our union." Without missing a beat, Chapman said, "I don't give a damn about your union. . . . I care about you." Chapman believes he and his management team have a sacred covenant to treat people well and return them home each day physically and emotionally healthy.[3] Barry-Wehmiller colleagues agree: 79 percent report that they believe that their company cares about them.[4]

Barry-Wehmiller's success shows that a culture of Caring strengthens the bottom line. Building relationships with colleagues makes work seem less like, well, work, and more like doing things with your friends. This is not only true at Barry-Wehmiller. A Society for Human Resource Management survey found that good relationships with coworkers and with one's supervisor directly increased motivation.[5]

Caring is not some new-agey, feel-good management trend. Academic research across industries shows that organizations that promote Caring create more value.[6] Both new-line and old-line companies have embraced Caring. PepsiCo's first guiding principle is Caring, online retailer Zappos includes Caring as one of its 10 core values, collaborative software company Slack lists empathy as a core value, LinkedIn practices "compassionate management," and Whole Foods articulates management principles using the word *love*.

As social creatures, human beings naturally form relationships. But at work we are advised to go against nature and avoid this. The Gallup organization has found that those who report having a best friend at work are substantially more engaged in the tasks they do than those who do not.[7] My field experiments in businesses across sectors have found a similar effect: Those who report that they work in a Caring environment are more productive and innovative.[8] Not only is there no reason to check your humanity at the door when you get to work; my studies show that having Caring colleagues increases engagement, productivity, and joy at work. Work is a community, and Caring makes the community work better.

Teamwork, including the challenge stress of eXpectation, stimulates the release of oxytocin, which increases empathy between work colleagues. Rather than inhibit this powerful response, organizations that encourage Caring tap into a fundamentally important human trait. The empathy that follows oxytocin release is also the foundation for ethical behavior,[9] reducing the need for a lengthy set of rules for employee demeanor, as discussed in chapter 5.

Rather than banning socializing at work, letting people take time to get to know others increases trust according to an MIT Media Lab study.[10] Supplying snacks and/or meals at work is also likely to build social bonds as it brings people together in a relaxed way and stimulates oxytocin release (which is one reason we have so many meetings during meals). You can encourage socializing by creating spaces for this to occur, from a Ping-Pong table to a coffee bar. Human beings want to get to know each other, so support rather than inhibit this. Don't worry, they still have challenging eXpectations to meet.

Deaths were inevitable. The United States' largest aluminum producer, Alcoa, had been doing things the same way for decades when Charlie Parry retired as CEO in 1987. Colleagues got hurt and even killed on the job. This was heavy industry, after all—injuries and deaths were inevitable. A few months after Paul O'Neill was appointed the new CEO, an 18-year-old Alcoa employee stepped over a barrier to clear a jam on a piece of moving equipment in an attempt to keep production running. He was killed and left a pregnant widow. O'Neill told his management team, "We killed him."

O'Neill was obsessed with worker safety from the moment he took the helm—often to the consternation of Alcoa's board of directors.[11] Lost productivity, insurance premiums, and health care were costing Alcoa millions of dollars a year. O'Neill thought that even one injury was one too many. Federal data showed Alcoa was in the top one-third of accident rates per employee in the 1980s. If employees were truly Alcoa's most valuable assets, why were they not being protected? O'Neill knew a culture change was needed and established a clear goal: zero injuries. The skeptics laughed.

To reach zero injuries, O'Neill created a team that would investigate every injury, find out what caused it, and change the production process to prevent it from happening in the future. The safety team reported directly to him and was empowered to make changes rapidly to protect colleagues. O'Neill then went a step further. He requested that every morning he was given a report listing each employee who was out sick and why. Once he had this data, O'Neill had nurses at the plant call everyone who was out sick each day to ask what the company could do to help the person get well. Was a ride needed to a doctor's office? Did someone need to pick up medication? Over the next decade, injuries at Alcoa dropped 93 percent, eventually scoring at the fifth percentile nationally.[12] Productivity soared and profits followed. During the 12 years O'Neill led Alcoa, its market capitalization grew from $3 billion to $28 billion.

Mining company Arch Coal copied many of the safety-first approaches used at Alcoa. Arch Coal is the second largest supplier of coal in the United States, generating annual revenues exceeding $4 billion. Its mantra is "A Perfect Zero" in which "every miner returns home safe and healthy." This Caring culture enlists all employees to spot risky situations before they cause harm. Arch's lost-time safety incident rate of 0.46 is less than one-fifth the industry average of 2.52.[13]

Emotional information. Physical safety is a must for a Caring culture. But Caring organizations also create emotional safety. As discussed in chapter 3, having high eXpectations for colleagues drives engagement. But when a supervisor does not understand that sometimes goals cannot be met, it shows a lack of empathy. This is particularly true if the colleague or team did their utmost to reach the goal. Caring is about creating an environment where colleagues' emotions are recognized and accepted as part of the human condition. Your colleagues are not robots, so do not treat them as such.

Even building a relationship with a single person can increase Caring throughout the organization. People who are disconnected from the community of colleagues are those who need extra support. A student of mine is a Catholic priest, and he told me about a member of his monastery who held a Ph.D. from an Ivy League university. As a young man, he taught at a prestigious institution and held high-ranking administrative positions in his order. After some time, he was directed to return to his home monastery in a small town. Rather than embrace him, his community thought him pompous, and this led to his isolation. One day the abbot invited him on a short journey. After driving a few miles, the abbot pulled over and said to him, "If nobody cares about you, I do," and gave him a hug. That simple act of Caring was the beginning of his journey back to community with the other priests.[14] A similar approach can be used in your organization to reintegrate the disconnected into the organization. Sometimes "difficult" people just need to be recognized and shown care.

Accepting colleagues as unique individuals with their own quirks and gifts means being patient with them. Although this is difficult for busy, highly focused people, patience demonstrates

Caring and accepts the weirdness in us all (patience is a virtue after all!). The essence of patience is endurance under difficult circumstances. When things get difficult, Caring colleagues are there for each other. As discussed in chapter 4, accepting that colleagues will complete projects differently is essential to stimulate innovation. From the perspective of a supervisor, this requires patience because people make mistakes as they figure out how to discharge a task. No one said this better than did Chuck Tanner, professional baseball player and manager: "There are three secrets to managing. The first secret is to have patience. The second secret is to be patient. And the third and most important secret is patience."

One way to build a Caring workplace is to focus on the emotions of those around you and articulate what you see. Emotions are a valuable information flow that leaders ignore at their peril. Rather than say, "Hi, John, how's it going?" when you walk by a colleague not really expecting an answer, practice reading John's emotional state. For example, "Hi, John, you look tired/happy/sad/worried/ today. How are you doing?" By articulating the emotions you see in others, you gain valuable information about the ability of team members to engage at work and the kind of coaching they need right now. More importantly, Caring shows that you value them as human beings. A Caring culture creates the conditions for trust and embraces diverse individuals as valued members of a team.

Code Lavender. Nearly 50 percent of physicians experience burnout during their careers, more than any profession, and nurses are nearly as high.[15] To help combat this, the Cleveland Clinic created an innovative program to make the emotions of their clinical staff apparent to colleagues. Similar to "Code Blue" alerts for medical emergencies, "Code Lavender" alerts tell hospital staff that someone is facing extreme stress or burnout.[16] Clinicians from technologists to nurses to physicians can request a lavender bracelet to wear after they have experienced a particularly difficult patient death or have worked many days in a row. Besides alerting colleagues that they may be emotionally fragile and to treat them with care, a team of holistic nurses provides massages and healthy snacks and can give spiritual support, mindfulness training, counseling, and yoga to those facing a Code Lavender.

In a small study at a Stanford University hospital, the proportion of clinical staff that felt unsupported by administrators fell from 24 percent to less than 3 percent after the Code Lavender program was started.[17] Though it was not measured, it is reasonable to assume that caregivers' motivation to perform at their best improved because of the program.

A laboratory experiment at International Islamic University in Islamabad, Pakistan, quantified the relationship between Caring and productivity. In this experiment, participants were asked to enter data for a stated wage. Prior to the work, the experimenters announced to one group that they would receive 17 percent more money than previously announced, while a different group was provided with personalized letters of appreciation for the work they would do. Importantly, these letters were not related to work performance (Ovation), but simply stated that the experimenters cared about the participants. Compared to the baseline treatment, the group who got the unexpected raise was 21 percent more productive. But the Caring intervention was more effective than money: Those who got letters of appreciation were 30 percent more productive. And of course, Caring costs nothing.[18]

Other Caring-building policies include paid time to volunteer in one's community, on-site day care so colleagues can visit their children at work, and permitting dogs in the office. My lab has shown that volunteering to help others, being around children, and dogs are all powerful oxytocin stimulants.[19] Once the brain has produced oxytocin, colleagues will have enhanced empathy for the next 30 minutes. This means that if you visit your child on a break from work, for the next 30 minutes your stress will be lower, your empathy higher, and you will be better able to collaborate with others. Besides providing food and snacks, consider supplying beer and wine to encourage colleagues to socialize after work. In my lab, I consider the beer budget money well spent because the researchers in my group get to know each other on a deeper level after work. Once you get to know someone, you naturally start to care about that person. This makes working with each other easier.

Attributes of Caring cultures. Long before Google made offering food and recreation de rigueur perks to attract the best engineers, Walt Disney did the same thing when he set up his animation studio in California in the 1930s. Disney had beer brought in at 4 p.m., set up volleyball courts, built a softball field, and provided Ping-Pong tables for employees to use. Disney played these sports and drank beer with colleagues, showing he really cared about them (more on this in chapter 9). Disney offered three days of paid sick leave a week with no questions asked. Vacations were flexible, pay was high, and stock bonuses were common. Disney wanted to create a culture of inclusion and Caring so his employees could achieve excellence. There is no doubt that they did.

Many other successful companies have been built around Caring. Tata Steel, part of the $100 billion annual revenue Indian conglomerate Tata Group, introduced an eight-hour workday in 1912, one of the first Indian companies to do so. Tata Steel soon offered benefits to colleagues, including no-cost medical care, pensions, training programs, and maternity leave. It even formed a management advisory group to facilitate colleague communication with supervisors.[20] Tata Group's motto is "Leadership with Trust." It's not just words: Tata is consistently ranked as one of India's most trusted companies.[21]

Caring can be done effectively off-site, too. Outdoor sports company Patagonia closes its retail stores once a year for a "field day." Colleagues vote on a place to go and an activity to do. Field days often include camping, hiking, biking, and fly-fishing. The field-day program was started to strengthen emotional bonds between team members while they enjoy the outdoors. Their passion for outdoor activities gives them a natural reason to build friendships, and field days enhance this. Many Patagonia retail employees also socialize outside of work on their own. They might hop on their bikes and go to a local brewery or find a rock to climb or head to the beach to surf on their day off. Building connections outside of work makes work feel more like play.[22]

Caring is even important for engineers. A Stanford University study of software engineers in Silicon Valley found that those who helped others with their projects not only earned the respect and trust of their peers, they were more productive themselves.[23] Google's studies of their best managers showed that these individuals "express interest in and concern for team members' success and personal well-being." In other words, Google's top managers are Caring. They understand that their colleagues have career goals as well as personal goals, and one's work should allow engineers to reach both of these. Even Google engineers have human needs.[24]

After a scathing 2015 *New York Times* article critiquing the lack of Caring at Amazon.com, CEO Jeff Bezos wrote that "any such lack of empathy needs to be zero." He asked employees to email him directly when they experience situations in which Caring was absent. Many Amazon investors and tech CEOs disagreed with the *Times* article. Peder Uslander, a Cisco Systems executive, said Amazon does not accept "C+ work" because it sets eXpectations high.[25] There is a natural tension that organizations have to calibrate between high eXpectations and Caring. Management experiments are the way to adjust this tension so that both factors fit into an organization's culture.

Helping cultures. Design firm IDEO creates a Caring culture by embedding helping into everything it does. IDEO has a high-Transfer culture, with senior designers advising project teams without dictating what should be done. At the same time, everyone is expected to cooperate with, and help, others. A Harvard University study found that 89 percent of IDEO colleagues help others with their projects. Who are these helpers? They are those who are viewed as most competent and trustworthy. IDEO has hired people and created a culture in which helping others solve problems is valued and enjoyable.[26] Just in case you wondered, there is absolutely no financial incentive to help others. Helping is simply built into how they brainstorm, prototype, and test designs.

David Kelly, IDEO founder, said he wanted to hire people who were his best friends.[27] This is a smart approach. It recognizes that working with those we like and care about makes work collaborative and enjoyable. Spending time in IDEO's offices, I could see that it hires people who have high emotional intelligence. Beyond that, IDEO's founders have created a culture of Caring that reinforces the human predilection to help others. When I gave a talk at IDEO about how Caring effectively builds a high-trust culture (while IDEO colleagues enjoyed a catered lunch), I saw general manager Tom Kelly nod his head in agreement. IDEO staffers do ethnographic studies of the needs, both practical and emotional, of their clients before starting the design process. They apply the same reasoning to building a Caring culture: They consider the needs of their colleagues in nearly everything they do.

One of the least empathic businesses are hospitals. Fifty years ago, most physicians would have been flummoxed at that sentence: Doctoring and Caring were inseparable. But today's managed-care, high-volume medicine increasingly depends on technology rather than humanity. Many patients are dissatisfied with their treatment, and care without a Caring touch is less efficacious (and increases the risk of malpractice suits).[28] Responding to these issues, Massachusetts General Hospital psychiatrist Helen Riess created a program to teach doctors empathy. Physicians with this training were judged by patients as significantly better at understanding their concerns, while patient outcomes improved and doctors were happier. Other medical schools have noticed. Empathy training is now part of the curriculum at Jefferson Medical College, Duke University, and Columbia University. Dr. James A. Tulsky, director of the Duke Center for Palliative Care, has found that doctors who were trained to be empathic inspire greater trust in their patients than those who were not.[29] Doctors can be taught empathy, just like organizations can be created around Caring.

Recreate and re-create. Re-creating is also part of Caring. By this I mean allowing people time to renew and refresh their lives. Besides unlimited vacation (chapter 5), paid sabbaticals are an effective way to refresh the energy of colleagues. Currently only 5 percent of companies offer this Caring benefit, but interest in sabbaticals is growing.[30] McDonald's was among the first companies to offer paid sabbaticals, starting in the 1970s. McDonald's employees earn an eight-week paid sabbatical for every 10 years of full-time continuous service. The sabbaticals are so highly regarded that McDonald's recently added an "Anniversary Splash" program in which employees get an extra week of paid time off on their five-year work anniversaries.[31] McDonald's wants colleagues on sabbatical to go on an adventure, learn a new language, or volunteer so they come back to work energized with fresh ideas.

Computer chip maker Intel also offers sabbaticals and had to put rules in place to make sure colleagues did not continue to work.

It bans colleagues on sabbatical from coming into the office or checking email and expects them to simply disappear for two months. Financial services companies, including Charles Schwab and Morningstar, have recently added paid sabbaticals. At Morningstar, colleagues are eligible for six weeks of sabbatical after four years of service. Joe Mansueto, Morningstar CEO, said his team tries to "create an environment for people to do their best work . . . [and] build a long career here."[32]

Lead-singer syndrome. Leaders have to concentrate on being Caring because of neurochemical changes that arise when one becomes the boss. In men and women, ascending to a leadership position causes testosterone to rise. Testosterone inhibits the brain's synthesis of oxytocin, the neurochemical that makes us care about others. You can spot those with high testosterone through what are called dominance displays. Think Donald Trump or Jack Welch in their $5,000 Armani suits and private jets. Rolling Stones guitarist Keith Richards calls this "lead-singer syndrome" when describing the self-indulgent behavior of front man Mick Jagger.[33] If you're the lead singer or CEO, your elevated testosterone can turn you into a jerk because testosterone tells your brain the world revolves around you. But extraordinary performance never happens alone. After all, Jagger does not play every instrument in the Rolling Stones. It's just that testosterone-fueled alphas cannot help but take credit for everyone else's work.

So what do you do if you're a CEO or division president or start-up founder? First, be mindful that you suffer from lead-singer syndrome. By being aware, you can choose to suppress the mindset that the company is your stage. Then take time to reflect on how your behavior affects those around you. Elicit honest feedback from trusted advisors, especially from those outside of your company. When CEO Michael Dell realized that most senior managers at

Dell Computer did not last more than a few years, one of his closest advisors told him why: No one wanted to work with him. A Dell survey in 2001 revealed that half of employees would leave if they got the chance. So Michael Dell hired an executive coach and worked to improve his social skills in order to become a Caring leader. He put props on his desk to remind him to be aware of what he was doing and to change his behavior. A plastic bulldozer cautioned Dell not to run over others; a Curious George stuffed animal was a reminder to listen to others. It worked. Turnover fell and teamwork improved.[34]

A student once asked Peter Drucker to tell him the most important thing in business. After a pause, Drucker said, "Good manners."[35] The brain saves energy by establishing default modes of behavior, so it takes effort to change habits. But the brain is also plastic, or changeable over time. If you are a leader, you can be Caring—if you put effort into it.

You can rein in testosterone and create a Caring culture by getting rid of dominance displays. If you are the senior person at a meeting, sit in the middle of the table rather than at the head to signal that everyone's voice will be heard. Ditch the expensive suits that only you can afford and instead wear the "uniform" everyone else wears. And how about flying commercial like everyone else rather than in a private jet. After all, you are all on the same team. Big corner office? Who needs it? Share an office with other managers; let them learn from you (and you from them).

Even office artwork can be a dominance display. When A.G. Lafley took over as CEO of Procter & Gamble in 2000, he had the expensive art hanging on the walls of the company's Cincinnati headquarters replaced with photographs of ordinary people from around the world. Most of these photos were of women, who are the primary purchasers of P&G products. This simple change signaled that Lafley was focused on "we" rather than "me."

In 2012, Apple CEO Tim Cook asked to be excluded from a recently instituted program in which Apple employees accumulate dividends on their vesting stock. Incredibly, he voluntarily gave up $75 million by having Apple not issue dividends to him. By passing on the cash, Cook avoided a dominance display. Let's be clear: Cook is well paid as CEO and with the stock he owns could earn half a billion dollars if he spends a decade at Apple's helm. Nevertheless, Cook was showing he's a team player and values fair treatment. Apple colleagues strongly support Cook as the first post–Steve Jobs CEO.[36]

Leadership is always personal. The Towers Watson Global Workforce Study of 32,000 employees from 29 countries found that Caring was the most important thing leaders can do to create a high-trust culture. Those who work with Caring leaders are 67 percent more engaged than colleagues whose supervisors do not care about them. Respondents said that Caring was more important to them than training, benefits, or salary. Towers Watson also found that Caring increases colleague retention.[37]

Serving others. Caring does not have to start at the top; everyone in an organization can find a way to offer others small kindnesses. On a Wednesday in 1977, about a year after it was founded, somebody at statistical analysis software maker SAS Institute put out a bowl of M&M's chocolate candies for staff who were working long hours building their next product release. It was a simple act of Caring. Snacks and food were provided to colleagues in subsequent years, and SAS began to emphasize work-life integration. "We'll take care of you if you'll take care of us" is the approach taken by SAS Institute co-founder and CEO Jim Goodnight.[38] Today, SAS Institute buys 22 tons of M&M's each year that are put in jars refilled every Wednesday.[39] It also is the world's largest privately held software company, with over $2 billion in revenue and 11,000 employees. The M&M's are a reminder to care about the welfare of others.

SAS Institute exudes Caring throughout the company. It offers on-site day care for 850 children of its employees at one-third the market cost, basic medical services at no cost, and asks colleagues to work 35 hours per week. Employee turnover is 2 percent, the lowest in the industry. Goodnight has said SAS Institute's culture is based on "trust between our employees and the company."[40] It is consistently ranked among the best companies to work for in the United States.

Just as SAS Institute's M&M's bowl was set up by a single colleague, Caring programs do not have to be designed from above. In the early days of Google, volunteer "tech advisors" offered to listen to colleagues with career concerns. These conversations evolved into broader discussions that helped people learn how to navigate life at Google. When Google's PeopleOps team evaluated the tech advisors program, they found that the most important part was that someone was listening. Here's the surprising part: The tech advisors themselves benefited from listening to their colleagues, reporting increased empathy for those with whom they work. Academic research backs up Google's findings. Managers who show warmth and affection have teams that perform better.[41] Google has now formalized this program, training "gurus" to listen to their peers and offer advice on leadership, sales, and even new parenthood. As one guru said, "You can automate many things, but you can't automate relationships."[42]

Apparel maker lululemon athletica has built Caring into its daily huddles. Managers take the first five minutes and ask colleagues to bring up anything that is keeping them from being fully present and to clear it away. People typically discuss personal issues or work challenges and receive feedback and support. lululemon leaders believe these interactions cause colleagues to see each other as whole human beings, not simply employees.[43]

Caring everywhere. A simple Caring intervention is to make a point to remember people's names. This can be hard in a large organization, but those whose names you remember will feel you care about them. Tom Gardner, cofounder and CEO of investment advisor Motley Fool, uses this technique to demonstrate Caring to his staff. "If you want to be a social and collaborative environment, you have to know everyone's name," said Gardner.[44]

Not only do colleagues crave Caring, but a Caring culture serves companies' interests. A study by Claremont Graduate University doctoral student Gregory Hennessy used a smartphone app to measure employees' moods and energy six times a day for seven days from 8 a.m. to 10 p.m. This provided a random sample of employee experiences during and after work hours that Hennessy then related to organizational culture. Those who work in a Caring organization, compared to an uncaring one, reported significantly greater creativity, were more engaged at work, and had higher energy. Hennessey also found that colleagues in Caring cultures experienced more Joy at work and a heightened sense of Purpose, topics we discuss in chapter 10.[45]

In a Caring culture, care flows from colleagues to customers. A recent study reported that 70 percent of customers chose new vendors because of a bad experience with a salesperson.[46] As a result, learning to be Caring can improve sales. The French pharmaceutical company Sanofi-Aventis trained a group of salespeople to be more empathic. Compared to a control group who did not get training, sales for the Caring group were 18 percent higher. American Express mimicked the Sanofi-Aventis program for some of its salespeople. Those trained to be more Caring saw sales rise 2 percent compared to those without training. Two percent may not sound like much, but it adds up to millions of dollars of additional revenue.[47]

Universal Caring. Working in a Caring culture is not just a Western aspiration. The brain's anatomy reveals that an emotional connection to others is an existential need for everyone. The receptors for oxytocin that make it feel good when people care about us are in evolutionarily old parts of the human brain. This means that our need for Caring has been part of human nature for eons. As social creatures, we do not function alone, and we function better when those around us care about us.[48] Companies outside the United States and Western Europe are starting to realize the importance of Caring.

Foxconn Technology Group is a Taiwanese multinational founded in 1974 and is one of the largest manufacturers of electronic components in the world. The company employs over 1 million people in mainland China. In 2010, 14 Foxconn employees in China committed suicide. This tragedy prompted founder and chairman Terry Gou to focus on building a Caring culture. The first thing he did was set up an around-the-clock, no-cost counseling center. Next, Gou and his staff required managers to attend training classes to teach them to be more Caring. In an effort to make the training stick, Foxconn launched a website called "Campus Loving Heart" to provide updates to managers on how to treat colleagues with care. Another insight gleaned from this incident is that people need to be embedded in communities, both at work and after work. While Foxconn had traditionally built factories in less-expensive rural areas, it is now establishing plants in large cities so colleagues can have a social life and social support nearby.[49]

Caring even matters when colleagues have to be fired. HopeLab, a nonprofit that creates technology products and games to improve people's health, dismisses colleagues in ways that are respectful, considerate, and even celebratory. For example, when letting go an employee who was a Michael Jackson fan, HopeLab staff created a "Thriller"-style flash mob. More typically, HopeLab has a party with balloons, beach balls, and food. Chris Murchison, the vice president of staff development and culture, has called this "the good in the good-bye." Murchison also helps former colleagues find new jobs by using his network. The pool of highly qualified talent is small, and treating everyone well, especially those who have to be let go, sends a clear signal inside and outside the organization that Caring infuses its culture.

"They're Not Employees, They're People" is the title of a 2002 article Peter Drucker wrote for the *Harvard Business Review*. Drucker argued that talented people are a competitive advantage in companies and must be treated well. He concluded, "The number one practical competency for success in life and work is empathy.[50]

The bottom line is that it is important to be nice to everyone. A study from Arizona State University's Thunderbird School of Global Management found that fully one-half of employees who were treated in an uncaring manner intentionally decreased the effort they put into their jobs, and one-third reduced the quality of their work.[51] We are social creatures, and it is vitally important to be sustained in a Caring community. Incivility, nastiness, yelling, and other Caring fails can have long-term effects on how people feel and how they behave. We all get frustrated, but a Caring culture reinforces that we must make an effort to recognize the humanity in colleagues.

☕ MONDAY MORNING LIST

▸ Practice becoming more Caring by verbalizing the emotions you see in colleagues.

▸ Avoid dominance displays by sitting in the middle of conference tables and inviting others to run meetings.

▸ Call every employee out sick every day to see what she or he needs to get well.

▸ Provide beer and wine for after-work socializing.

▸ Invite colleagues to bring dogs to the office.

Chapter 8

Invest

Organizations Invest in colleagues when they enable whole person growth. Invest explains 72 percent of organizational trust.

Fully one-third of human resources managers surveyed in 2015 said that retaining colleagues is their number one concern. Everyone knows that employees are mobile. About one-quarter of employees say they will look for a new job in the next year. Some are chasing a higher salary (23 percent), but nearly as important is the desire for a better opportunity (19 percent), a failure to be appreciated (16 percent), and unhappiness with growth opportunities at their present organization (13 percent). Employers underestimate the importance of personal and career development on employee retention, vastly overestimating the importance of salary and benefits.[1] As Josh Bersin, founder and principal at Bersin by Deloitte, has said, "The war for talent is over, and the talent has won."[2]

It is actually worse than that. A third of employees believe their current job skills inhibit their productivity and are holding them back from career growth. Who's to blame? Three-fourths of employees say they do not have a clear professional development path, and 31 percent don't feel their employer has trained them adequately.[3] Accenture's 2015 survey of college graduates finds that "employers' lack of commitment and investment in entry-level jobs" is the number one reason that highly sought-after STEM (science, technology, engineering, and math) graduates eschew working for large companies.[4] For those in their 20s, the most important factor in selecting a workplace is professional development.[5]

Even though companies worldwide report that retention and engagement is a "highly urgent" concern, the average company spends only 31 hours a year training colleagues.[6] High-Invest organizations, as defined by the Association for Talent Development, do much better, averaging 49 hours of training annually.[7]

Across industries, Invest is nearly always the lowest of the OXYTOCIN factors. Many organizations Invest in colleagues only as an afterthought, signaling that they do not trust colleagues enough to provide them with new opportunities. Invest is not as simple as increasing training hours for employees or sending them to a conference. Invest recognizes that volunteer-employees have multiple goals at work and in life. By facilitating growth of colleagues as human beings, Invest provides the foundation for a long-term commitment to the organization.

This chapter introduces the Whole Person Review, which, in conjunction with the previous factors discussed in the book, radically changes the annual review process into a forward-looking guide to growth. We see how companies such as SAS Institute, Zappos.com, and theater operator Decurion Corp. Invest in colleagues in order to increase organizational performance.

Just as fully engaging in life requires a movement toward greater well-being, the evidence shows that fully engaging at work requires more than just job skills.[8] If we want colleagues to bring their heads and hearts to the job, we need to also consider how their professional, personal, and spiritual development interact with each other—something I call whole person development.

Philosophers and psychologists agree. Aristotle thought that personal growth came from the acquisition of practical wisdom and believed this was the foundation for human flourishing. Psychologists from Carl Jung to Abraham Maslow to Martin Seligman have provided evidence confirming the importance of growth broadly understood if one is to thrive. Now, neuroscience experiments are deepening our understanding of why having rich experiences is important, showing that the brain continually reshapes itself.

Among the most exciting findings in neuroscience in the last decade is that the dogma of inevitable neuron death as we age is false. We do lose some neurons as we age, but Fred Gage and his collaborators at the Salk Institute have proven that adults can produce new brain cells. Using a very clever transdisciplinary approach, Gage found that people, even those of us with gray hair, make new neurons. This process can be accelerated if we exercise vigorously and are challenged cognitively. New neurons do not arise everywhere but appear mostly in brain regions associated with learning, memory, and emotions.

Being challenged at work—think here of the role of eXpectation—affects the brain in the same way as a challenging bicycle race or running a 10K does. When our bodies and brains are working hard, the brain Invests in remodeling. This includes a reduction in peripheral fat, increased muscle mass, and some newly minted neurons. In the economy of the brain, there is no free lunch. In work my colleagues and I did evaluating "brain-training" technologies, we found that one can get better at specific tasks if they are done over and over. The bad news is that a couple of weeks after you stop practicing, you are not much better at the new task you practiced, or at doing other tasks. Doing crossword puzzles is not going to stave off Alzheimer's disease, but exercising and being challenged at work just might.[9]

Organizations that Invest in colleague health are likely to get a positive return. Workplace wellness is a $6 billion a year industry in the United States that continues to grow.[10]

Colleagues who participate in wellness programs have higher job satisfaction and less absenteeism and consume less in health-care costs. Making a financial commitment to colleagues' health by, for example, setting up an on-site gym shows that the organization is committed to colleagues beyond the eight hours a day they work. A culture of wellness keeps colleagues at work and increases energy during work, so it is a smart investment.

The production of new brain cells, called neurogenesis, occurs at a modest rate in healthy adults. But it can be inhibited as well. Being bored, sedentary, chronically stressed, and lacking sleep make your brain sludgy. This is why challenging work is good for your brain. Setting high eXpectations followed by an Ovation that includes recovery and solid sleep are the ingredients for neurogenesis. For most of us, work is where we are challenged the most, often surmounting challenges with supportive teammates. But this is only half of the Invest equation. The other half is maintaining family ties and having the capacity to reflect on what one is doing and where one is going.

Looking forward. As discussed in chapter 3, waiting for the annual review to give feedback to colleagues seldom increases performance because the brain needs fast feedback loops to learn. Companies are recognizing that annual reviews do not work and are, frankly, dreadful. Microsoft, Adobe, Accenture, Deloitte, and that "rank and yank" stalwart General Electric have phased out annual reviews. Projects rarely run on an annual cycle, so why review colleagues this way? Instead, these companies are moving to a rapid-feedback coaching model. As Donna Morris, head of human resources at Adobe who transitioned the company away from annual reviews and ratings, said, "It's a process that looks in the rearview mirror, that's focused on what you've done a year ago." These companies have stopped asking supervisors to supply annual ratings of direct reports because ratings are subjective, inconsistent, and often biased.[11]

In 2013, Google moved from an unwieldy 41-dimension performance rating to a transparent, single 1-to-5 rating. Google also asks individuals themselves to identify one thing they can do better. This is meant to initiate a conversation with one's supervisor about additional training and goals. Googlers get constant feedback as they leave one team to join another (the average team size is nine and is together for three weeks).[12] Deloitte's approach has team leaders ask four forward-looking questions in its new quarterly reviews. These questions focus on what they would have colleagues do in a future project rather than what they think of that individual. This is supplemented with weekly check-ins that Deloitte has called a manager's "killer app."[13]

Reviewing the whole person. Google puts job candidates through a grueling process before they are hired. Once found, Google does not want to lose these "unicorns." Instead of firing those who do not perform as expected, Google Invests in raising the skills of the bottom 10 percent and offers extensive training opportunities for everyone else. More than 100,000 Googlers take classes taught at Google each year.[14] In addition, as discussed in chapter 3, Google separates supervisors' discussions of professional development from salary discussions. Laszlo Bock, Google's head of People Ops, believes that connecting skill acquisition to salary inhibits learning.[15]

If managers are setting eXpectations and having Ovations when goals are met, traditional annual reviews are not necessary. If managers are empowering colleagues with Yield and Transfer, traditional annual reviews are not necessary. And if managers practice Caring for those around them, the salary-focused annual review is not necessary. This is where the Whole Person Review comes in.

The Whole Person Review is forward looking and focuses on growth toward goals and the steps needed to reach them. It assesses professional goals as well as colleagues' personal and spiritual goals. By spiritual I mean anything outside of work and family. If you do not like that word, you can substitute *recreational* or *emotional*, but I'm using *spiritual* to denote those activities that let us reflect on who we are now, who we want to be, and how we are living our lives. Research in positive psychology has shown that answering these questions is necessary to truly thrive.[16]

An effective forward-looking annual review should assess how the organization improves the lives of colleagues. Yes, you read the sentence properly. High-trust organizations serve their colleagues and, in turn, colleagues volunteer to further the organization's goals. If the company you work for reduces your quality of life, you should volunteer your employment elsewhere. This is the reason organizations with great cultures are high in Invest: They are making commitments to colleagues as whole people.

Before you begin someone's Whole Person Review you should already know about his or her performance. Whether productivity is subpar or this colleague is knocking the ball out of the park, this should already have been discussed and a plan to fix problems or celebrate successes has already been made. Performance needs to be part of daily and weekly feedback—not part of an annual review.

Three questions. The Whole Person Review is based on three questions: Are you growing professionally? Are you growing personally? Are you growing spiritually? The science shows that if any one of these is stalled, a colleague is heading for frustration and poor performance at work.[17] Without movement forward, motivation stalls and performance follows. The Whole Person Review is an open-ended conversation, always done in private.

When managers ask these three questions, they are aligning themselves with the thinking of Peter Drucker: "For a superior to focus on weakness, as our appraisals require him to do, destroys the integrity of his relationship with his subordinates."[18] Instead, Drucker advocated open-ended and forward-looking evaluations of employees in his 1967 classic *The Effective Executive*.

To assess forward-looking professional growth, I ask, "Am I helping you get your next job?" This provocative question permits a discussion of whether the organization has invested enough in developing a colleague's professional skills. Someone's next job might be with one's present organization or it might not be. In a world of volunteers, helping someone get a job at another company can be advantageous. You might collaborate with her new company on a project, or you might rehire her in a couple of years when she's gotten additional experience elsewhere. My secretary has told me for years, "I'm perfectly happy and plan to retire with this job." Great, but I want to make sure she's not bored and wants to move to a different position before her performance lags.

Google maintains a listserv of Googlers who have left to work for other companies. This keeps them in touch with happenings at Google and lets people at Google stay in touch with them. Often, after a stint elsewhere, they come back to Google with new skills and experiences. These boomerang employees often have valuable training Google did not pay them to acquire. Some businesses even "lend" employees to other companies on a long-term basis to expose them to new experiences and to build relationships between organizations.

Work-life integration. To assess personal growth, I ask, "Are you and your family happy?" Find out if the location at which a colleague works is acceptable to one's spouse and children, if the spouse is satisfied with his or her job and other activities, and if the children are doing well in school. It is important to be ahead of potential crises by inquiring in advance; this is certainly the preferred option to having a stressed-out colleague quit suddenly because of family discord. This question also taps into whether a colleague has achieved a reasonable work-life integration.[19] Integration is different than balance since many colleagues endowed with Yield and Transfer work at home, or in coffee shops, or at night as it suits them, their teams, and their families. Discussing how to integrate work and life is valuable when assessing if personal growth is occurring.

Sometimes during a review people tell me they are happy with their present job and do not want a promotion because it enables the personal dimension of life to flourish. That's important for them to understand and for me to know. What people do at home feeds back on professional performance and vice versa. We shouldn't pretend that it doesn't.

The reciprocal is also true: Promoting a colleague because he or she has been with the company for a long time is nearly always a mistake. A great front-line colleague may not be a great manager, and a great manager is not necessarily going to be a great executive. The skill set to be successful is different for customer-facing employees, managers, and C-suite leaders. Recognizing that some colleagues are growing their personal lives by holding their professional lives at a given level acknowledges the importance of noncareer priorities.

Life goals. The final dimension of the Whole Person Review is spiritual growth. You can ask this question any way you like, but the core issue is whether a colleague is developing as a human being. What are the colleague's outside-of-work passions? How is he or she making the planet and other people better? If spiritual development is not nurtured, it eventually leads to disengagement and sadness—and those are not performance boosters.

Running is the spiritual practice for Beth, a member of my lab. During her Whole Person Review, she mentioned how important this was to her. I suggested that she come in at 10 a.m. twice a week so she could run in the morning. She was not only happy I had asked, but was thrilled we could make this happen. She was so happy she said she'd like to be a member of my lab for the rest of her life (and I hope she will). Occasionally when we are deeply immersed in a project, I get a 3 a.m. email from Beth because her passions are fed both at work and in her life outside of work.

At retailer lululemon athletica, every employee receives coaching and is asked to set personal, professional, and health/activity goals. The goals are then posted publicly in each store. This approach is meant to generate conversations that allow colleagues to support each other in reaching goals. The equivalent of the human resources department at lululemon is called "People Potential" to signal that its role is to help associates reach their life goals.[20]

Doubling development. Personal and professional development can be done at the same time by, for example, subsidizing college tuition. Starbucks recently offered to pay for online college classes for any of its 135,000 employees who work 20 hours a week or more. While many who finish college will stop working at Starbucks, some may value this Investment in them and move up the ranks with a deep understanding of the company. Or you can Invest in colleagues by letting them try out new roles at work. Facebook has a "hack a month" program that lets engineers try a new team and project briefly to see if they want to move.[21] Consultants Booz Allen Hamilton have an internal recruitment system called "Inside First" that uses career coaches that work with colleagues to attain the skills needed to fill open positions. Just asking a colleague about his or her next job opens up a discussion about education, training, conference attendance, and how to attain professional goals.

In a world in which valuable colleagues can volunteer to work elsewhere, Invest also creates talent ambassadors who can recruit people to work for the organization because they love what they do. Just as word of mouth is the most powerful consumer marketing, colleagues who evangelize for the company are the best talent recruiting. I saw this during a study we did for Zappos.com: About half of the Zapponians who participated in the study on a nonwork day wore Zappos logo shirts. When I asked why, they said that Zappos's values resonated with their own and that working for Zappos was a big part of their identities. Zappos has created raving fans who volunteer to work for them. And people know about it. In 2013, Zappos received approximately 30,000 job applications for 350 positions. In 2014, it got rid of job applications altogether. It now recruits from referrals from existing employees using a software platform so Zappos "ambassadors" can get to know them.[22]

Good-bye review. Dumping the annual review can be stressful, so let's talk about how to do this. I worked with a large southern U.S. employee-motivation company that was engineering a turnaround. The Ofactor survey showed what everyone knew intuitively: Invest was nonexistent. This explained why many of its best employees left for companies with better career opportunities. A new executive team took over and held town hall–style meetings to listen to the concerns of their colleagues and communicate (Openness) that they were going to fix problems identified in the data.

I worked with the new leadership team to develop a strategic plan that focused on increasing eXpectations, Yield, and Invest. An Invest budget was approved to fund colleague training programs, provide career counseling, and support external training opportunities. The company also adopted the Whole Person Review. When the president of the company announced the end of annual performance reviews at an all-hands meeting, colleagues whooped and gave him a standing ovation. Managers who previously had to do reviews were as relieved as front-line colleagues. A year after these changes were made, energy is high, sales are up, and people are genuinely excited about coming to work again.

As with every intervention, changing Invest should be seen as an experiment. A financial services company I worked with had very uneven Ofactor scores across divisions. A particularly low-trust division was in insurance. Turnover was high because insurance sales was viewed as a dead-end job. Invest was particularly low (40th percentile) since, as a senior vice president told me, "These people are not going to stay." I gently suggested that the causation might be reversed and that I could help him discover a set of policies to improve Invest.

The management experiment we designed would use employee turnover as the key outcome we sought to affect. The first part of the plan was to meet with colleagues in insurance to discuss the changes. During this meeting, a career ladder was presented that showed how colleagues can progress from insurance sales to other positions in insurance, to other positions in the company. Approval was given to Invest in employees' professional growth by offering training that would more rapidly move people from working the phones to going up the ladder. I recommended that supervisors be trained to actively engage in career planning and mentoring with direct reports. This last point was not enacted because the VP told me, "No one had the time." As an alternative, I recommended hiring a mentor/career coach/life coach as a clear signal that the company was Investing in colleagues and building long-term commitments to them.

While this management experiment was being implemented, the Great Recession of 2008 hit, and the company's financial position was compromised. The experiment was never fully implemented, so the company couldn't track its impact on reducing turnover and increasing job performance. But the approach was right: Run management experiments on the lowest Ofactor components, test their efficacy at changing key outcome measures, and then do it again.

Innovative companies have used a variety of methods to Invest in colleagues. These can vary from offering perks to make one's life easier (dry cleaning, car servicing, or take-home dinners) to classes that focus on developing new interests or aptitudes. Office designer Herman Miller's headquarters in Holland, Michigan, has invested in a coffee bar staffed by baristas from 8 a.m. to 10 a.m. Zappos had an amazingly kind and warm full-time life coach on staff for years, August Scott, whom I met while assessing Zappos's culture. She helped Zapponians figure out how to save for a house, navigate work with a new baby, or finish one's college degree. And, she'll just listen if someone is having a bad day (or a good one). She recently retired but has been replaced by other life coaches at Zappos.

Games and training. Professional training is a core part of Invest. Most businesses on *Fortune* magazine's Best Companies to Work For list spend significantly more on training than do other companies. Baristas at Starbucks receive at least 24 hours' training in the first four weeks after being hired. There are classes on coffee history, drink preparation, customer service, and retail skills. Every staff member also has to attend a four-hour workshop on brewing the perfect cup of coffee. The Container Store offers full-time associates 263 hours of formal training in their first year, compared to the industry average of about 8 hours, and more than 100 hours of training in subsequent years.[23]

Package shipper UPS gamified its driver training in 2010 to great effect. It collaborated with the Massachusetts Institute of Technology, Virginia Tech, and the Institute of the Future to build a high-tech, next-generation training facility called UPS Integrad that is designed to teach millennials about UPS's delivery processes. The facility offers 3-D simulations, webcasts, and traditional classroom instruction. After initial training, new hires play a video game that places them in the driver's seat of a UPS truck and tests their ability to identify and avoid obstacles. Then trainees start driving real trucks. They must make five deliveries in 20 minutes to level up. This engaging approach to training reduced the costs of driver injuries by 56 percent, package delivery costs 12 percent, and produced an efficiency gain of 7 percent. UPS estimated that the return on the investment from the program was 9.2 percent. This is not to mention fewer driver injuries and happier customers. UPS's 102,000 drivers worldwide are among the safest on the roads, logging more than 3 billion miles per year with less than one accident per million miles driven.[24]

Nap time. Besides additional training, many organizations Invest in sleep. Companies such as Zappos, Google, Procter & Gamble, HubSpot, and Facebook have Invested in napping rooms. A recent estimate puts lost productivity due to sleep deprivation at $63 billion a year.[25] Naps improve cognition and the brain's ability to remember new facts by increasing a neurotransmitter called acetylcholine in the hippocampus. The hippocampus is the key structure that moves short-term memories into long-term knowledge. Naps also flush toxins from the brain, reducing accumulated damage to neurons as we age. Many businesses have new parents or travelers who are chronically short on sleep. Nap rooms recognize this (Caring) and Invest in a solution. Even a 10-minute nap can be enough to improve cognition.[26]

The go-go days of 100-hour workweeks in investment banking are over, as many of the brightest college graduates see technology rather than finance as the future. To keep the best talent, Goldman Sachs created Goldman Sachs University to Invest in professional growth. But it also provides guidance on taking time off. Employees are forbidden to be in the office between 9 p.m. Friday and 9 a.m. Sunday, and working at home during this period is strongly discouraged. Staff are also encouraged to take at least three weeks of vacation a year. In another Invest program, Goldman Sachs has dumped the two-year renewable contracts for new analysts it used to offer; analysts are now hired without a termination date. The co-head of investment banking at Goldman Sachs said, "The goal is for our analysts to want to be here for a career. We want them to be challenged, but also to operate at a pace where they're going to stay here and learn important skills that are going to stick. This is a marathon, not a sprint." Goldman Sachs even started a mindfulness meditation class for its associates. A mindfulness program at Aetna Insurance was estimated to have saved about $2,000 per employee in healthcare costs and to have increased productivity by $3,000 per person.[27]

Productive rest. Studies support Goldman Sachs's guidelines to reduce overwork. A 2015 analysis of more than 600,000 people found that those working more than 55 hours a week have a 33 percent higher incidence of stroke and a 13 percent higher likelihood of heart disease compared to people working 35 to 40 hours a week.[28] The United States is among the worst offenders for excessive work, averaging 1,768 hours of work per year, while the French and Germans work less than 1,500 hours a year. More than a third of American employees do not even use all their vacation days, and one-half report that they do not have time for more than a single break on an average day.[29] Yet a Towers Watson study found that those who take at least a brief break every 90 minutes report 28 percent more focus than those who take just one break or no breaks at all. They also have 30 percent better health and well-being.[30] Even Pope Francis advocates moderation at work. In his 2014 Christmas greeting to the cardinals, bishops, and priests who work at the Vatican, he faulted their excessive work, saying, "Rest for those who have done their work is necessary, good, and should be taken seriously."[31]

In 2001, British-Dutch consumer goods company Unilever had reached a breaking point. Senior executives were leaving in droves because of stress and overwork. In response, Unilever created "Lamplighter," a health and well-being program that helped executives manage their energy and performance by reducing chronic stress. Its early success led to a rapid rollout to Unilever's 172,000 employees around the world. The program assesses physical and mental health and creates individual scorecards that team members use to develop personal work-life integration plans. These plans include exercise and nutrition goals and even psychological counseling if needed. Unilever's analysis showed that for every £1 spent on the program, £3.73 was returned in higher productivity.[32]

Committing colleagues to work 40 hours a week is a way to Invest in creating a stable and healthy workforce. Going all out for 40 hours a week but no more has been called the "Firm 40." Companies like mortgage lender United Shore Financial Services that use Firm 40 expect the parking lot to be empty at 6:05 p.m. and that work is not taken home.[33] I have worked at companies where no one leaves before 8 p.m. and others in which the office clears out at 5 p.m. When I knew I couldn't go home before 8 p.m., inevitably I shopped online, took breaks, and was less engaged for the long workday than if I knew the lights went out at 5 p.m. Having a policy that people go home at 5 p.m. or 6 p.m. Invests in having high-energy colleagues.

Invest portfolios. Many high-Invest organizations actively facilitate professional and personal development for colleagues. SAS Institute, the statistical analysis software company we discussed in chapter 7, Invests in its colleagues in many ways. These include an almost limitless set of classes to acquire skills and advice from career mentors. Another important Invest decision at SAS is minimizing the use of contractors and instead hiring the people the company needs. This commits colleagues to SAS and allows SAS to commit to them. SAS also Invests in personal development, offering help finding care for elderly parents, financial assistance and paid leave for adoptions, on-site sports and recreation facilities, a beautiful campus with resident artists, and healthy food. SAS is winning the war on talent: It receives 200 applications for every opening.[34]

DaVita Healthcare Partners founded DaVita University to offer teammates nearly 700 in-person and online courses in professional and personal development. DaVita's data show that of those who attend courses, only 12 percent leave the company, compared to 28 percent for colleagues who do not. DaVita spends over $10 million per year on professional and personal development programs, producing over 1 million hours of content. DaVita also provides medical and dental benefits, profit sharing, and various forms of educational assistance, including tuition reimbursement. This focus on the whole employee consistently lands DaVita on *Fortune* magazine's World's Most Admired Companies list.[35]

Theater operator and real estate developer Decurion Corp. is designed around whole person development. "Decurion provides places for people to flourish" is the first statement on its website. President Christopher Forman said, "We see business as a place of wholeness, connection, excellence, and meaning."[36] It does this by Investing in its 1,100 "members" (not employees) personally, professionally, and emotionally. Professional growth is encouraged by moving people between positions and letting everyone in the company know when members acquire new competencies (Ovation). Proficiency is reinforced by having members teach others skills. Personal growth is promoted by aligning individual interests and goals with projects at work. Decurion managers are trained to be coaches and servant leaders, leading personal discussions with members that focus on goals (eXpectation) and encouraging risk taking (Yield). Decurion has even created a 10-week Transfer-focused course called "The Practice of Self-Management" as another way to Invest in its members.

A high-Transfer approach to training and development allows self-managing individuals to choose what they want to learn. This can be implemented by having a variety of learning opportunities offered at varying times so colleagues can attend according to their interests. When people manage their own time, they can choose to Invest in gaining new knowledge and skills during the day, at night, or on weekends, in a classroom or online. A number of companies have peer-led learning that has been called "teach a colleague a skill." It's okay if the skill is not a work skill. Teaching colleagues how to give a TED talk, or dance the salsa, or sing builds the social ties that undergird trust. This is particularly important as the share of routinized jobs in the United States has fallen to 25 percent. Everyone needs to Invest in updating skills.

You can Invest in colleague engagement and retention by providing broad training opportunities and by using the forward-looking Whole Person Review. The best-run organizations make Invest a priority and extend training beyond professional skills so that their colleagues have a fulfilled and satisfying life. This ensures that they continue working for the organization for the long term.

☕ MONDAY MORNING LIST

▸ Develop a forward-looking Whole Person Review.

▸ Offer or subsidize additional education and training.

▸ Provide wellness options on-site or subsidize them off-site and track their impact on productivity.

▸ Develop peer education programs to stimulate professional and personal growth.

▸ Hire a life coach/mentor to counsel colleagues during work hours.

Chapter 9

Natural

An organization is Natural when leaders are honest
and vulnerable. Natural explains 82 percent of organizational trust.

During a visit to office designer Herman Miller's headquarters in
Holland, Michigan, I spotted Curt Pullen, Herman Miller's North
American president, sitting in a (really nice) open office typing on
his laptop. I hadn't seen Pullen in a year, so I stopped by and asked
if I could interrupt him. He said he needed a break from building
next year's strategic plan, and we went to Herman Miller's coffee
bar and grabbed lattes. Several employees said hello, and Pullen was
friendly and considerate. He embodied leadership behaviors that
neuroscience shows are important to creating a trusting culture: He
was warm, competent, but also casual (no tie) and relaxed. He knew
everyone's name. He's in charge, but he does not need to constantly
remind those around him about his position.

Pullen embodies Natural. While we spoke, he was approachable,
open, and attentive; interested in hearing my sometimes-contrarian
opinions; and genuinely kind to those around him. We talked about

our children and our aspirations and how these are integrated into our career goals. I felt privileged to spend an hour with Pullen, who is responsible for a billion-dollar division.

Being vulnerable. As social creatures we need leaders. A Natural leader is one who accepts responsibility for mistakes and includes others in wins, who knows the organization at every level, from the front lines to the executive suite. A leader's qualities explain up to 70 percent of the engagement of followers.[1] This chapter presents the science and practice of being a Natural leader.

Because human beings are good at identifying snake-oil salesmen (and saleswomen), leaders of high-trust organizations must themselves be trustworthy. They must not only talk the talk of trust, but they have to embody trust themselves. Neuroscience experiments from my lab prove that an effective way to build trust is for leaders to show vulnerability. I'll pause here for the collective gasp to dissipate.

Leaders are not omniscient gods but people trying to do the best they can for their organizations. Natural leaders embrace their vulnerability; they let it show. Vulnerability is a sign of strength because it signals teamwork rather than dominance over others. Jim Whitehurst, CEO of open-source software maker Red Hat, has said, "I found that being very open about the things I did not know actually had the opposite effect than I would have thought. It helped me build credibility."[2] Google team manager Matt Sakaguchi found the same thing during an off-site meeting to discuss team frictions. Matt revealed that he had been battling stage four cancer for several years and was not getting better. This vulnerability encouraged other teammates to open up about difficulties they were facing. By the end of the meeting, the frictions had melted away, and Matt was enthusiastically embraced as an effective leader.[3]

Asking for help is anathema to most leaders; they seem to presume that asking, rather than demanding, shows weakness. Experiments from my lab have shown that being vulnerable releases oxytocin in observers, motivating them to work harder on the organization's objectives.[4] Asking for help from volunteer-colleagues should be a daily practice for a Natural leader because this taps into the evolutionarily old human impulse to cooperate. Asking for help is crucial when one has implemented Yield and Transfer; demanding outcomes dictatorially is leading by fear, while asking for help while setting clear eXpectations is leading through trust. Steven Mollenkopf, CEO of semiconductor manufacturer Qualcomm, said his most valuable leadership attribute is to admit "I don't know the answer here."[5]

An exception to this rule comes during a major crisis; in such a case, leaders may have to demand changes. But in nearly every other situation, admitting that you don't have all the answers is an effective way to engage colleagues. Asking for help also removes the burden of omniscience from leaders. The organization's strategic plan is the leadership's best evaluation of the way to move forward. It is, necessarily, an experiment. If parts of it fail, Natural leaders own the failure and try something different.

Natural biology. The science of Natural is fascinating. Those with high social status, including leaders of both sexes, have chronically high testosterone. As discussed in chapter 7, testosterone increases selfishness and diminishes empathy. Both of these shortcomings undermine trust. It is not only behavior but physicality that advertises high testosterone: The brains of those who are tall and muscular have been imbibing testosterone since they were young. After I made a C-suite presentation at a Fortune 50 financial services company, I was struck by how tall the men and women were. "This is where the alpha males and females work," I recall thinking. Alphas are found in executive suites everywhere. In the United States, 14.5 percent of men are six feet tall or taller. Among male CEOs of Fortune 500 companies, 58 percent are six-plus-footers.[6] The inevitable conclusion is that leading an organization diminishes one's ability to be a Natural leader.

How do you fight your biology? Start by being aware of the issue. With self-awareness comes an ability to observe and modify one's reflexive behaviors. It requires effort to inhibit the impulse to be self-absorbed, but it can be done. The brain is an energy-intensive organ and saves calories by setting up default pathways that resist change. This is the neuroscience behind habits. Changing habits is difficult but can be accomplished if you make a conscious effort and receive feedback from those around you. Or consider using an executive coach, as Michael Dell did, to break old habits and set up new ones.

Imperfections and pratfalls. Another surprising behavior of Natural leaders is embracing their imperfections. This is not as crazy as it sounds. Psychologists have discovered that one's likability increases after one makes a mistake, dubbing this the "pratfall effect." For example, President John F. Kennedy's popularity increased after he accepted responsibility for the botched 1961 Bay of Pigs invasion of Cuba.[7] This "pratfall" showed he was trying hard to make the best decisions and needed the support of the American people to be a more effective leader. Experiments as far back as the 1960s have found that people are put off by others who seem to be perfect but warm to those who appear flawed like themselves.[8] Leaders who need to fortify their veneer of perfection often come off as insecure.

Owning one's mistakes is proof of trustworthiness. Contrast President Bill Clinton's weaselly statement, "It depends on what the meaning of the word *is* is," when questioned by a grand jury about his sworn statements regarding his relationship with Monica Lewinsky, or Richard Nixon's feckless admission, "Mistakes were made," when questioned about the Watergate break-in, to Steve Jobs's remark, "Sometimes when you innovate, you make mistakes. It is best to admit errors quickly, and get on with improving your other innovations."[9] Which leader is more secure in his position? Which inspires more trust and confidence? As Peter Drucker said, "Rank does not confer privilege or give power. It imposes responsibility."

An important caveat, though, is that leaders who show imperfections engender trust only if they are regarded as being competent. Incompetent leaders who ask for help from others undermine perceptions of reliability.

Leaders model culture. Organizational culture typically reflects the behavior and personality of the founder(s) as well as the current leadership. Leaders set the agenda for the organization, enhance or undermine an organization's culture, and serve as exemplars of culture internally and externally. Management consultant McKinsey & Company found that about one-half of efforts to change organizational cultures fail because leaders do not model new behaviors, or because colleagues create insurmountable barriers to change.[10] This squares with my experience: To effect real culture change, top leaders must be fully on board.

Leadership quality impacts engagement even for those who largely self-manage, such as physicians. Forty-six percent of medical doctors report being burned out from overwork. The Mayo Clinic found that the degree of burnout was reduced by 3.3 percent for every 1-point increase in physicians' estimation of executives' leadership effectiveness (on a 60-point scale).[11]

Like any skill, you can become better at being a Natural leader. The remainder of this chapter provides examples to follow. Even if these behaviors may not seem natural to you, if you do them enough, they will become second nature.

Being authentic. Natural leaders let others see their authentic selves. Whatever you seek to hide comes out eventually, so save the energy and let loose. At an all-hands meeting in late 2013, Zappos CEO Tony Hsieh dressed up as Miley Cyrus and danced onstage, mimicking Cyrus's odd and embarrassing Video Music Awards twerking episode. Everyone laughed (as did Hsieh), and the mood was relaxed as he outlined Zappos's strategy for the next year.

In a deeply personal approach to authenticity, Apple CEO Tim Cook enhanced his reputation as a Natural leader when he announced he was gay in a 2014 *Bloomberg Businessweek* article.[12] Cook accepted that some people might be put off by his sexual orientation, but his willingness to publicly share his personal life won accolades from nearly everyone.

I encountered a wonderful way to show one's authentic self at a market research company in Argentina. When the company president handed me his card, it had a photograph of him as a child sitting on a pony. What a candid way to open oneself to others. All the other employees had pictures of themselves as children on their business cards, and all were as embarrassing as was the president's. I learned that the company had found that the cards made colleagues more approachable and reminded everyone that they are just big kids. We're all human, so embrace your weirdness.

Listening to everyone. As we have discussed in earlier chapters, leaders need to take in new information and broadly share information. Bidirectional information flow is easier when senior leaders are available and open to meeting with colleagues. Mutual fund giant Vanguard Group's former CEO Jack Brennan arranged regular lunches with employees to discuss their concerns. Eating together reduced the trepidation of having a face-to-face with the boss and let employees see Brennan as a team member. Brennan has said, "People look to [the leader] and they will emulate what that person does, good or bad."[13] Natural leaders connect to their colleagues at all levels. Do you know the names of your housekeeping staff? They are as valuable as human beings as anyone else at work and have important front-line information.

The opposite tack was taken by a southern U.S. business services company I advised on its turnaround. It had a large campus with conference rooms named for retired executives. Why not name a conference room after a janitor who had served the company for 30 years? Acknowledging people shows that everyone is important when seeking to reach the organization's goals.

The way Natural leaders get to know colleagues is by letting themselves be known. Share your values and experiences, discuss why this organization is so important to you, and build emotional ties with others. You can even greet colleagues with a hug to stimulate oxytocin production. Once the oxytocin flows, those around follow you.

First names. A leader is more approachable without the dominance display of putting titles around one's name. In 1999, personal computer maker Lenovo Group was going global. But this Chinese company had a very Chinese culture. People would only speak in hierarchical order. Tea was served at every meeting. And titles were paramount. CEO Yang Yuanqing was called "Chief Executive Officer Yang" by everyone. To stimulate the flow of information and ramp up innovation, Yang sought to change Lenovo's culture. One of the first things he did was to post himself in the lobby of Lenovo's Beijing headquarters for more than a week wearing a "Hello, my name is Yuanqing" sticker and shaking hands with everyone who walked through the door. He asked employees to address him by his first name. He also changed the official language at Lenovo to English.

The changes worked. Lenovo grew from an Asian-only brand to a global behemoth shipping more PCs than any other company in the world. Lenovo generates over $46 billion in annual revenue.[14] Ovation is also part of the culture. In 2012, Yang received a $3 million bonus. Rather than take it, he distributed it to 10,000 of Lenovo's employees. *Barron's* magazine consistently names Yang one of the World's Best CEOs.[15]

Working up front. There is no need to stay locked in the corner office. Leaders need to acquire information, and the most valuable information is obtained firsthand. Herb Kelleher, founder of Southwest Airlines, regularly loaded luggage with the baggage handlers, served drinks to customers on flights, and showed up at the airport in weird hats or funny clothes to make people laugh and relax. *Fortune* magazine rated Kelleher among the best CEOs in the country because he spent time with customer-facing colleagues and had a ball doing it.[16] In a similar way, executives at the Cleveland Clinic, one of the best hospitals in the United States, are required to do "leadership rounds," joining medical staff working with patients. Every employee at Zappos.com spends at least 10 hours answering customer service calls during the busy Christmas season—even CEO Tony Hsieh. Hsieh does not identify himself as CEO when people call, and he sits with the Customer Loyalty Team when doing his 10 hours like everyone else.

Soon after Jorge Mario Bergoglio was chosen to lead the Roman Catholic Church, taking the name Francis, he decided to have lunch in the Vatican's employee canteen. Pope Francis stood in line with a tray to get his food and then sat at a table with Vatican warehouse workers and discussed soccer. Francis is very humble, a trait that makes him easily approachable.[17]

Spending time on the front lines to see how the organization works has been called leading from the rear. Natural leaders recognize that they are enablers of others' success, not the organization's omnipotent commander. Natural leaders do this by bringing others into the spotlight. Vocalist James Maynard Keenan of the art rock band Tool performs from the back of the stage, while the band's drummer and bass player are up front. Keenan often faces the backdrop or the sides of the stage rather than the audience. He's the band's lead vocalist, but his workmanlike approach literally shines the spotlight on the others.

Honesty to trust. Natural leaders maintain credibility by being honest. If you pretend to know everything, eventually the holes in your knowledge show and undermine everything else you do. Verizon CEO Lowell McAdam puts it succinctly, saying that as a CEO, "integrity is your brand."[18] It can also save your health. Participants in a study who were asked to try not to tell a lie for five weeks reported fewer sore throats, headaches, and nausea than those in a control group who lied as usual.[19] Honesty is the best policy because it is cognitively simple; it takes fewer scarce neural resources to be honest than to lie or evade the truth. All lies are eventually revealed, so why risk it?

The bottom line is that honesty engenders trust. Even hardnosed former General Electric CEO Jack Welch has come around to this view, saying, "Leadership 2.0 is all about . . . truth and trust."[20]

Warm leadership. A global survey by the *Harvard Business Review* found that respect for others was the most important leadership behavior influencing commitment to the organization's goals.[21] Natural leaders set high eXpectations without being nasty. Netflix Chief Executive Reed Hastings has said that his company doesn't need "brilliant jerks" because no one wants to work with them, concluding that their "cost to effective teamwork is too high." Carly Fiorina, former Hewlett-Packard CEO, has said, "Abrasive never works."[22]

One way for leaders to show respect for colleagues is to start and stop meetings on time. I started doing this with my meetings some years ago, and very quickly the norm of doing things on schedule permeated everything we did. If you have implemented Transfer, another way to show respect is to keep meetings as short as possible and even to make them optional. An exception would be an all-hands meeting, but otherwise, if colleagues are managing their own projects, then they should decide if a meeting is sufficiently valuable to them to attend. Forcing people to attend a meeting signals that you know how to manage their time better than they do.

Salary rules. Part of respecting others is recognizing their skills and paying them appropriately. Or, equivalently, not paying leaders exorbitantly. In a 2011 letter to the Securities and Exchange Commission, Peter Drucker wrote, "I have often advised managers that a 20-to-one salary ratio is the limit beyond which they cannot go if they don't want resentment and falling morale to hit their companies."[23] In 2015, average CEO pay for companies in Standard & Poor's 500 (S&P 500) index of the largest U.S. companies was $13.8 million, while the average median employee salary at these companies was $77,800, a ratio of CEO to employee salary of 204.[24] So much for the Drucker rule.

A Natural exemplar is Jim Sinegal, who built the second-largest retailer in the United States by focusing on fairness. As founder and CEO of Costco, he earned $350,000 a year, an amount even the Costco board said underpaid him. His salary was 10 times the average Costco employee's pay, and two times that of the highest paid store managers. Jim would wear his Costco name tag every day and worked in stores at least once a month. He constantly demonstrated that he was a team player.[25] People genuinely liked Jim and worked hard for him. One sign of this is that theft at Costco stores (customer and employee) is one-tenth of the industry average.[26]

Information about salaries, bonuses, and stock options eventually leaks out to the organization. If the leadership is overpaid, especially when asking others to tighten their belts, trust is undermined. In fact, the more CEOs are paid, the worse their companies perform. And the longer these highly paid CEOs are at the helm, the more their organizations suffer, both in stock performance and accounting performance.[27] The "don't overpay" mandate is counter to the conventional wisdom that to get the best performance you have to pay for the best executives. This is the Theory X view of motivation. Nearly every study undertaken on motivation supports Theory Y: Intrinsic motivation is more powerful and longer lasting than cash. Very high salaries can induce testosterone-fueled overconfidence in leaders' decisions and prevent them from listening to advice from others. If leaders are paid in grand excess compared to their colleagues, "me" dominates "we."

High-trust organizations privilege "we" over "me." Leaders need to check their egos at the door, roll up their sleeves, and get in the trenches with everyone else. If you have built a company or have been a senior leader long enough, you are likely to have an equity interest. Fair enough, but if you want to sustain trust, keep your salary reasonable.

Shared leadership. Communications and marketing firm Ketchum reports that the CEO-as-celebrity leadership style is rapidly disappearing in favor of a "leadership by all" culture that empowers employees at every level.[28] An organization that practices Transfer necessarily requires that everyone serve as a leader—and as a follower. When trust is high, each person assumes a leadership role at different times and in different places, so Natural is important for everyone, not just those in the C-suite.

Natural establishes a culture where everyone assumes leadership duties. This can be done by offering formal leadership training at all levels of the organization. But it can be done more subtly by actions that show that the "customers" of the senior leadership are front-line employees. Leaders of some companies wash employees' cars or bring in breakfast or shine employees' shoes, like Dan Cathy, CEO of Chik-fil-A, does. Humility is extraordinarily appealing; it shows that everyone, from the CEO to the housekeeping staff, is on the same team.

Checklist. I fly a lot, and I love everything about airplanes. In the early days of commercial air travel, pilots were "skygods" who could do no wrong and never took advice from others, including their first officers. As the volume of commercial air travel increased in the 1950s, these skygods started crashing planes and killing passengers at an alarming rate.[29] This led to extensive studies of the behaviors that differentiate good pilots from bad. The guidelines for a responsible pilot are a great checklist for how to be a Natural leader, so I'll reproduce them here:

A. The *Ineffective* Pilot-in-Command

▸ Conforms with the stereotypes of the "macho pilot" and the "right stuff"

▸ Does not recognize personal limitations of crewmembers who are under stress or who are faced with emergencies

▸ Fails to make use of available crewmember resources— skills, knowledge, and experience

- Does not have sensitivity to the problems and reactions of other crewmembers

- Is likely to foster a tense flight deck atmosphere

- Is unlikely to foster a flight deck atmosphere based on team coordination among crewmembers.

B. The *Effective* Pilot-in-Command

- Recognizes that crewmembers have personal limitations

- Recognizes that crewmembers have diminished personal decision-making capabilities in emergencies

- Encourages other crewmembers to question decisions and actions

- Is sensitive to the fact that personal problems might affect crewmembers' performance

- Openly discusses personal limitations

- Recognizes the need for the pilot flying the aircraft to verbalize planned actions and procedures

- Recognizes the role of the captain in training other crewmembers

- Recognizes that the flight deck atmosphere must be relaxed and harmonious

▸ Recognizes that management styles must vary with the situation and the make-up of crewmembers

▸ Emphasizes that the captain is responsible for coordinating crewmember responsibilities.[30]

That's a succinct list of what to do and not to do as a thoughtful, compassionate, Natural leader. It also recognizes that at times, leaders have to step up and take care of situations when others cannot. A Natural leader is a servant leader.[31] A servant leader's primary focus is helping members of the organization be successful and fulfilled human beings. A recent study found that servant leaders are more trusted by their colleagues than are Masters-of-the-Universe leaders.[32] Natural leaders reinforce a culture of trust by bringing their passion, strengths, and weaknesses to work every day. A culture of trust cannot be sustained unless leaders fully embrace it and are themselves trustworthy.

Former Herman Miller CEO Max De Pree wrote, "The first responsibility of a leader is to define reality. The last is to say thank you. In between, the leader is a servant."[33]

☕ MONDAY MORNING LIST

▶ Spend at least one day a month working the front lines.

▶ Ask for help, rather than demand outcomes.

▶ Commit to listen twice as much as you speak.

▶ Be vulnerable by sharing your feelings with others.

▶ Remember to show respect to everyone; to make this stick, fine yourself $10 every time you treat someone badly and donate the money to charity.

Chapter 10

Joy =

Trust × Purpose

Joy is created from trust and transcendent purpose.
The correlation between Trust × Purpose and Joy is
0.77.

Arbejdsglaede. Only the Scandinavian languages have a word for Joy at work; in Danish it is *arbejdsglaede.* What do the Danes know that most of the world does not?

To find out, my team and I spent a week in Las Vegas. We weren't spying on Danes at a business convention; we were holed up in a loft in downtown Vegas running a neuroscience experiment on employees from one of the happiest companies in America, Zappos.com. Did Zapponians have *arbejdsglaede* because managers hired inherently happy people or because the culture at Zappos made *arbejdsglaede* possible? Let's drop the Danish and just call this Joy.

I drove with researchers from my lab in a rented panel van to Las Vegas with syringes, tubes for blood, dry ice, and wireless sensors to measure cardiac rhythm, vagal tone, and palmar sweat. Zapponians are unusual, and we hoped that collecting brain activity while they worked would reveal what made them so joyful. If having passionate, committed colleagues comes down to hiring right, then culture may not matter that much. Previous chapters have discussed the importance of culture fit when hiring. But if Joy comes from putting a certain type of people in any old culture, then cultures need only include what these special hires need to be successful. Trust is still going to matter, but perhaps not as much as finding the right people. This chapter shows that the answer to whether high-engagement colleagues come from making the right hire or having the right culture is that both are necessary.

This chapter also explains why effective cultures cause colleagues to experience Joy at work. And we'll add another catalyst to achieve high performance: Purpose. The positive feedback between Purpose and Trust is captured in the equation Joy = Trust × Purpose. Once we have dissected this equation, I present data from a number of experiments that support this relationship. If there is nothing else you remember from this book, remember the equation Joy = Trust × Purpose. It is a succinct statement of how to create a culture of high engagement. When colleagues regularly experience Joy at work, you have a great culture.

Where is maximizing shareholder value in all this good feeling? Shareholders nominally own the company, and their interests—often over the short term—are supposed to be paramount. While many economists still preach this gospel, it confuses correlation and causation. The value of a company increases as the result of doing the right things: building a culture of high engagement and innovation, taking good care of customers, and being good stewards of the resources entrusted to the company. Embracing the improper causation, that managers should focus only on maximizing shareholder value, has resulted in shortermism, extraordinary excesses in compensation, ill-advised corporate mergers, and renouncing responsibility to the two most important constituencies of a company: colleagues who work there and customers who pay their salaries.[1]

Former General Electric CEO Jack Welch, a proponent of maximizing shareholder value when he ran GE, has become a vociferous critic of this view, calling it "the dumbest idea in the world. Shareholder value is a result, not a strategy."[2] Many thoughtful business leaders now agree with Welch, and many disagreed with the notion of maximizing shareholder value when it was floated in the 1970s. In 1979, Quaker Oats President Kenneth Mason wrote, "Making a profit is no more the purpose of a corporation than getting enough to eat is the purpose of life. Getting enough to eat is a requirement of life; life's purpose, one would hope, is somewhat broader and more challenging. Likewise with business and profit."[3] I call the larger set of goals that an organization accomplishes its transcendent purpose.

Fundamentally, organizations exist because they improve the lives of customers, colleagues, and communities. This is an organization's transcendent purpose. The only reason clients pay for a company's services is because it makes their lives better. Every organization can identify and measure its transcendent purpose and assess whether it is being fulfilled.

Transcendent purpose should be distinguished from an organization's transactional purpose. Every business has processes that allow for efficient transactions, from ordering materials to producing goods and services to their delivery to customers. The small-p transactional purpose is the quotidian "doing" of business that is vitally important to turning a profit. Transcendent purpose is a bigger concept: how the organization serves people and their needs. I'll use a capital P to denote this larger notion of Purpose and drop "transcendent" when the meaning is clear.

Not about happiness. Neuroscience makes a nonobvious prediction about high-trust organizations: Trust combined with Purpose results in Joy at work. Experiments from my lab and others show that working in a high-trust culture modestly increases Joy. Trust effects Joy through the interaction of oxytocin and dopamine (chapter 1), making it feel good to be around trusted team members. Being trusted by others also keeps chronic stress levels low, eliminating a drag on Joy. But understanding the value the organization creates for society, its Purpose, provides a second oxytocin stimulus. Helping others—even at a distance—is a powerful oxytocin booster.[4]

The science here is subtle, and many organizations have missed the point: Organizations should not try to make people happy at work. Joy is the *result* of working with trusted colleagues who have a transcendent purpose. The OXYTOCIN factors are designed to challenge colleagues to meet important goals. It is that striving that research has shown produces a sense of accomplishment.[5] Joy arises naturally when people want to be at work and are challenged and recognized for what they do. In one of comedian Chris Rock's routines, he talks about dropping out of high school and working as a dishwasher at a Red Lobster restaurant. All day he stood at a sink scrapping shrimp off of people's plates. He said he knew it was a job because time passed achingly slowly. Now he has a career and he never has enough time because he has so many exciting projects; in his words, "When you have a career there just ain't enough time in the day."[6] The monologue was hilarious, and you get the point: Careers produce Joy; jobs seldom do.

Neurologist, psychiatrist, and survivor of the Nazi death camps Viktor Frankl wrote, "It is the very pursuit of happiness that thwarts happiness." This holds at work and outside of work. Joy results from the process of being trusted and the autonomy it enables, but it depends critically on embracing the organization's transcendent purpose: how a business or nonprofit serves the needs of customers, students in school, or citizens in one's city. Frankl called this "striving to find meaning."[7]

The two great management thinkers of the 20th century, Peter Drucker and W. Edwards Deming, both considered knowledge of an organization's Purpose essential to achieving high performance. Drucker wrote, "In our society of organizations, it is the job through which the great majority has access to achievement, to fulfillment and to community."[8] The medieval philosopher and Catholic saint Thomas Aquinas said it similarly: "There can be no joy in living without joy in work."[9]

Finding Purpose. A Deloitte/Harris Poll shows there is a serious worldwide Purpose deficit. Sixty-eight percent of employees and 66 percent of executives said that their organizations do too little to create a culture of Purpose. Here's where it gets really interesting: For those who work in high-Purpose organizations, 91 percent said their companies have a history of strong financial performance, 94 percent said their companies have outstanding customer service, and 79 percent said they are satisfied with their jobs. The corresponding values for organizations low on Purpose? Only 66 percent have strong financial performance, 63 percent have great customer service, and only 19 percent of employees are satisfied with their jobs. Only one-half of those surveyed even knew their organization's Purpose.[10]

You must do two things to capitalize on the power of Purpose. First, you must clearly and succinctly identify your organization's Purpose. Second, you must ensure that colleagues experience

Purpose. Many companies have Purpose statements, and I'll discuss these below, but having a longer Purpose narrative can be more powerful than simply a short phrase.

To find your organization's Purpose, start with its founding myth: Why did the founders put their livelihoods at risk to start the company? Has that vision been sustained? Does every colleague in the organization share this vision? Purpose is best communicated as a story in which the founders and their struggles are featured. Purpose narratives should describe how the founders sought to improve the lives of others: customers, community members, and the world. They necessarily focus on other people's needs, not on self-aggrandizement.

If you do not want to use your organization's founding myth as the basis for a Purpose narrative (if, e.g., your organization has merged several times), try the chronological opposite: What did the founders want to be remembered for at the end of their careers? Or: How does the current CEO want to be remembered? Next, ask what the organization is doing to create this legacy. This question gets at the deep "why" of the organization, and a Purpose narrative can be built from it.

A culture of Purpose on purpose. If you want maximum impact, Purpose narratives must be repeated until they penetrate every part of the organization. During a visit I made to LinkedIn, the San Francisco–based networking and recruiting company, every employee I met used LinkedIn's Purpose statement in the first five minutes of our conversation. Their Purpose is to "connect the world's professionals to make them more productive and successful." This outward-focused statement captures how their work improves people's lives. While it is not a story, it is succinct and memorable. "Culture and values are LinkedIn's most important competitive advantage," Jeff Weiner, LinkedIn's CEO, told me.

Each business unit uses LinkedIn's Purpose to assess whether a project should move forward or not. Weiner added, "You can never repeat these things too much."[11] He is right: Purpose has impact when every colleague knows it.

Purpose narratives with passion and turmoil are better remembered than stories that just state the facts. Passionate narratives are also more likely to incite action.[12] Management theorists Jim Collins and Jerry Porras give the example of British Prime Minister Winston Churchill's speech to the British people on the eve of World War II as an effective Purpose narrative. Churchill did not say "Beat Hitler." He built a story of a heroic struggle, saying,

> Hitler knows he will have to break us on this island or lose the war. If we can stand up to him, all Europe may be free, and the life of the world may move forward into broad, sunlit uplands. But if we fail, the whole world, including the United States, including all we have known and cared for, will sink into the abyss of a new Dark Age, made more sinister and perhaps more protracted by the lights of perverted science. Let us therefore brace ourselves to our duties and so bear ourselves that if the British Empire and its Commonwealth last for a thousand years, men will still say, 'This was their finest hour.'[13]

Now that's a Purpose narrative.

Building Purpose narratives. Many organizations regularly create new Purpose narratives to reinforce their reason for being. The best Purpose narratives use human-scale stories that follow a hero's journey—that is, a story with tension and emotion that features ordinary people doing extraordinary things.[14] Those in the narrative can be colleagues from the organization or they could be customers in need who were helped by a member of the organization. You can find the plot points in your Purpose narrative by asking five "whys": Why do you sell this product or service? Why do you operate as you do? Why is anyone interested in what you have to offer? Why should you continue doing this? Why is it important? Leaders should collect these stories and deploy them for maximum effect.

Trader Joe's monthly newsletter to employees regularly includes stories of colleagues who went above and beyond for customers. A newsletter in the early 2000s related the story of a Trader Joe's employee who left his post to jump-start the car of a customer in the rain. The customer was so delighted that she wrote CEO Doug Rauch a letter thanking him for creating an environment that truly puts customers first—even after they have made their purchases. Rauch told me that Trader Joe's Purpose is to delight its customers; they just happen to do this by selling food. The jump-starting-a-customer's-car story was circulated so other colleagues would be energized by it.[15] When organizations have a Purpose, they become causes, not just places for transactions.

My lab has researched the neurobiology of narrative for a decade in order to understand why some communications are persuasive. We have shown that because we are social creatures, our brains love stories inhabited by people to whom we can relate. Good stories develop tension and have conflict and nearly always include a transcendent purpose. They feature a fallible but heroic character who must struggle to do something extraordinary. Tellingly, our research has demonstrated that when such stories cause the brain to make oxytocin, we empathize with the hero, and this engenders a desire to emulate that person, changing our attitudes, opinions, and behaviors. Stories "hack" the brain by providing exemplars that tell us about the human ability to reach new heights. Part of our research on narrative was funded by the U.S. Department of Defense. It wanted to equip Special Forces fighters with another powerful weapon to motivate cooperation: stories. Our findings are now used to train soldiers at Fort Bragg. If stories with Purpose inspire voluntary cooperation in war zones, they will work in your organization.[16]

Living Purpose. Purpose narratives delivered by customers can be powerful because they have personally experienced something transcendent. The University of Michigan, like all higher education organizations, has an advancement office in which people in phone banks—often students—call alumni to request donations. Most people say no or hang up without saying anything or yell at the caller. An intervention by then Michigan graduate student Adam Grant, now a professor at the University of Pennsylvania's Wharton School, brought in a student who was attending Michigan on scholarship so he could tell the students in the phone bank how much their work was impacting his life. During the next month, donations went up 171 percent.[17] Those on the phones experienced the organization's Purpose and remembered this compelling narrative while they worked.

The Purpose of Walt Disney parks is to create happiness for its guests. This Purpose is shared with cast members during their first day at orientation and is repeated continuously through videos, newsletters, and by stories shared by leaders. Everyone, no matter the person's role, is expected to pick up trash, wish guests wearing a birthday pin a happy birthday, and answer guest questions because that is what it means to work at the Happiest Place on Earth. Disney Parks colleagues live Purpose simply by walking around their parks.

Another way Disney Parks reinforces their Purpose is by having midnight events where colleagues in teams act like detectives, finding clues to solve a puzzle. Disney Parks runs this event every year, and it is a high point for colleagues.[18] Disney has created a ritual that lets colleagues experience the happiness they seek to deliver to others. Other companies use rituals to strengthen teamwork and communicate Purpose. DaVita Healthcare holds the DaVita Olympics, in which teams compete with each other in light physical activities and perform skits and songs to see who wins the gold medal. Aaron Hurst, founder of nonprofit Taproot, advocates thinking of Purpose as a verb: The organization has to do something about it.

Rituals reinforce Purpose and build Caring ties between colleagues. My lab has shown that group activities such as marching, singing, and meditating strengthen social ties by causing oxytocin release.[19] Caring comes more easily when there is a transcendent purpose at stake. There are always things to do at work that are unpleasant, but most people are motivated to do them when they understand that it serves the needs of others. My lab spent nine months running a complicated neuroscience project for the U.S. Air Force, working 10-hour days six days a week. It was exhausting. When my team was tired and unhappy, I reminded them that we were doing impossibly hard science in an effort to save military lives. That was our Purpose narrative. For months, my team and I soldiered on, eventually collecting 10 terabytes of data and completing the most audacious integrative neuroscience project on interpersonal trust that we, or probably any other lab, had ever done. Knowing why we were working so hard helped carry us through the difficult times.

Broadcasting Purpose. Purpose narratives can be broadcast beyond the organization's walls to engage colleagues and customers. In 1997, when Steve Jobs rejoined Apple Inc. as interim CEO, he launched a $100 million ad campaign, "Think Different," while Apple was laying off 31 percent of its 4,100 employees and restructuring the company. Apple had only enough money to keep the doors open for 90 days, but Jobs insisted it had to advertise. The campaign was outward focused, aspirational, and did not mention computers at all. It featured iconoclastic rebels, including Mahatma Gandhi, Thomas Edison, and Pablo Picasso, and was meant to inspire Apple's employees first, and only secondarily to attract customers.[20] In 2013, Apple CEO Tim Cook took a page from Jobs's playbook and launched an ad campaign called "Designed by Apple in California" that was aimed at inspiring Apple's employees and was later released on the Internet. "This is why" was the tagline. It tapped into Purpose directly by showing how hard Apple colleagues work to make their products beautiful, simple, and innovative. Apple is proud of its engineers' hard work, and it wanted every Apple employee (and its customers) to feel pride in their Purpose.

Sometimes Purpose can come from outside the company's core mission. Beautologie, a plastic surgery and medical spa company, did not have a clear Purpose until it decided to offer free tattoo removal at its clinics. It has now helped more than 500 former gang members escape their pasts and get better jobs and live better lives. The staff is proud of what they have done because they are involved in something beyond beauty and profit.[21] Maritz Travel instituted a Purpose program to report sexual trafficking in an effort to end this horrendous practice in the myriad countries in which it does business. Employees at Maritz and Beautologie report that helping people live better lives is highly motivating.[22]

Storydoing. The use of Purpose narratives to clarify business goals has been called "storydoing."[23] Tom's Shoes's exemplifies storydoing with its easy-to-understand "One for One" model. It donates a pair of shoes to a needy child for every pair someone purchases. This means that customers live Tom's Shoes Purpose story with every purchase. These are stories about children, poverty, and goodness that are alive throughout Tom's Shoes's ecosystem. Recently, the company has moved into eyewear, using the "One for One" model to improve children's vision. Tom's Shoes is no longer a shoe company—it is a storydoing company.

Another storydoing company started after an accidental find. In 1982, an Austrian toothpaste salesman named Dietrich Mateschitz was on a business trip to Thailand and arrived heavily jetlagged. Locals directed him to a store selling a concoction called Krating Daeng that truck drivers and laborers used to stay energized. The drink worked, and Mateschitz realized that young, athletic people would be a significant market for this tonic. Mateschitz contacted the local manufacturer and they formed a company to produce and distribute the drink. From the beginning, Mateschitz and his partners saw their drink as part of a lifestyle for those living life to the fullest. You may have already guessed that Krating Daeng translates into English as Red Bull. Through its sponsorship of extreme sports like skydiving, ice climbing, and white-water rafting, drinking a Red Bull makes you feel like you have joined an elite group of athletes who do the impossible.[24] Spending a weekend at the same hotel as a group of Red Bull colleagues in the Sierra Nevada mountains, I can attest that the company lives its Purpose proud and loud.

Other storydoing companies include Disney, Target, Starbucks, American Express, and Apple. An analysis comparing financial results for storydoing companies and traditional storytelling companies found that from 2007 to 2013, the former had an annualized revenue growth rate of 9.6 percent compared to 6.1 percent for the latter.[25]

Inclusive Purpose. It is important for an organization's Purpose to be inclusive. Consider eBay's Purpose: "Through commerce, we create value that helps each of us pursue a better life and forge human connections that enrich our shared experience." The use of "we" and "us" clearly signals that its goal is not to maximize profits or stock price but to serve all of humanity. Service is essential in Purpose narratives. Colleagues at organizations that have a clear and well-communicated Purpose use "we" much more than "me." Athletic gear maker lululemon athletica's Purpose is to develop leaders who will help "elevate the world from mediocrity to greatness." This is both inward and outward looking, aspirational, and grand in scope.

Agrochemical giant Monsanto's Purpose statement is simple and direct: "Feed the world.[26] It captures why it does what it does. It is a call to action; it is storydoing. No fancy words, easy to understand, completely inclusive. The data show it works: Monsanto was named company of the year by *Forbes* magazine in 2009, and revenue exceeds $15 billion.

Harley-Davidson reinvigorated its Purpose narrative for its 100-year anniversary in 2003 by crafting a memoir of Harley-Davidson designer William Godfrey "Willie G." Davidson, grandson of the founder. It commissioned a book in his voice using archival information and photos, and packaged it with a black rubber cover and the same aluminum logo that goes on the company's gas tanks. This was an engaging way for employees and customers to learn about the company. It was human scale, heroic (Harley-Davidson nearly went bankrupt in the late 1970s, and Davidson put up his own money to buy back the company from AMF Inc. in 1981), fun, aspirational, and allowed the company to highlight why it is passionate about motorcycles. Consider creating artifacts like Harley-Davidson did that capture Purpose in a tangible way for your organization.

Purpose narratives do not have to be handed down from the C-suite (though executives need to be fully supportive); they can come from front-line colleagues. In 2014, CEO John Veihmeyer of the Big Four accounting firm KPMG asked colleagues to write down what motivates them at work. Amazing Purpose statements appeared, such as "I promote peace," "We protect our nation," and "I advance science." The success of this program led the company to define its Purpose in two sentences: "Inspire Confidence. Empower Change." But putting this on its website would just be window dressing. Colleagues had to feel it and live it. To make this happen, KPMG created a series of videos that showed how it helped to resolve global crises, ranging from the negotiations to end World War II to the Iranian hostage crisis to the election of dissident Nelson Mandela as president of South Africa. The release of the videos was followed by posters put in offices that showed how colleagues have improved the lives of their customers, communities, and the world.

In searching for its Purpose narrative, KPMG discovered that its colleagues were excited to contribute their own Purpose stories and wanted to read others'. To do this, it built an app called "10,000 stories" so colleagues could share their viewpoints. It was a big success. As of this writing, 42,000 stories have been collected.

The results? Two years into their Purpose initiative, 89 percent of KPMG colleagues say they work for a great organization, up from 82 percent before the program. Those who worked for supervisors who communicated Purpose were 50 percent more motivated to perform at the highest level than those whose leaders failed to discuss Purpose, and they were half as likely to leave the company. KPMG's leadership-development program now includes a module that helps colleagues develop compelling Purpose narratives. The increased pride at KPMG coincided with a 17- position jump on *Fortune* magazine's 2015 100 Best Companies to Work For list.[27] Veihmeyer said, "I've always believed that culture is the most important dimension of any CEO's responsibility to an organization."[28]

Insurance giant AIG began developing colleague-inspired Purpose narratives after an office in South Korea created one for itself. The South Koreans shot a video that described why serving their customers made them happy at work. Even though they made it for their own use, the idea caught on at many of AIG's offices worldwide. AIG leadership loves these videos and encourages offices to make them.[29] Total cost to AIG: zero. Virgin America colleagues recently did the same thing, dancing in a video when a new office opened; Virgin CEO Richard Branson praised the video when he saw it.[30] In a similar way, Loma Linda University Medical Center asks clinicians to share extraordinary experiences they have had during patient care. It put these into an annual book called *LOV* (*Living Our Values*), stories that all colleagues receive.

Helping others. There is abundant evidence that Purpose is essential to an individual's psychological well-being. At work and outside of it, colleagues focus, flourish, and are more resilient when their activities have meaning.[31] Even when times are difficult, people who identify with a Purpose in their lives are more satisfied than are those who do not have a clear Purpose. "If there is meaning in life at all," Viktor Frankl wrote, "then there must be meaning in suffering."[32] Yes, sometimes we suffer at work, suffer to meet deadlines, suffer to achieve excellence, but when this is done alongside trusted teammates and with Purpose, the struggle can produce Joy. A study that asked participants to keep their hands in ice water as long as possible found that people could endure the pain longer if they had a friend with them.[33]

Many organizations provide opportunities for colleagues to be of service to others by sharing their resources and expertise. Google has a program to encourage Googlers to get annual flu shots. When they do, Google pays for a child in a developing country to be vaccinated for meningitis or pneumonia.[34] DaVita has a program called "The Bridge of Life" that lets teammates participate in starting dialysis clinics in underdeveloped countries.[35] LinkedIn has a "mission day" when colleagues teach high school kids to code. This is part of a larger initiative called "LinkedIn for Good" in which teammates work with military veterans and nonprofits to help them transition into private sector jobs. When LinkedIn builds new buildings, it showcases "LinkedIn for Good" in art hung on the walls so everyone can see its Purpose.

Other companies have signaled their transcendent purpose by incorporating as public benefit corporations (B corps). Natural cleaning products company method changed to a B corp in 2013 to emphasize its Purpose internally and externally. B corps are 46 percent more likely to have satisfied and engaged employees than other businesses.[36] To be recognized as a B corp, a company must be certified that it meets high standards of social and environmental ethics while still earning a profit. B corps have higher transparency requirements than traditional corporations and must report their impact on all stakeholders, not just shareholders. The highly diverse group of companies that have chosen to be B corps communicate their commitment to social and environmental goals. In 2015, the $50 billion annual revenue consumer goods company Unilever said it is considering pursuing B corp status, so the movement embracing Purpose is growing.[37]

Late in his life, Peter Drucker argued that nonprofit organizations should serve as a model for for-profit companies because nonprofits depend on a culture of Purpose.[38] Volunteers choose to engage with nonprofits because they believe in their Purpose. For-profit businesses should seek to similarly engage their volunteer-employees. To quote Drucker, "What is needed in this world today is not primarily wealth. It is vision. It is the individual's conviction that there is opportunity, energy, purpose to his society."[39] Everyone is happy when the stock price goes up, but long-term motivation requires Purpose.

Testing the effect of Purpose. My lab has run experiments to understand why Purpose is motivating and how trust reinforces it. The first test we did was a neuroscience study in which requests for peer-to-peer microloans for female African entrepreneurs from the nonprofit Kiva.org were modified to include or exclude Purpose. For example, a microloan might be requested to reduce violence against women by providing more female employment opportunities—a transcendent purpose. We obtained brain data from 122 people while they viewed loan requests in order to identify if Purpose motivated more loans, and if so, why. We found that 45 percent more participants made loans to projects with Purpose, and these projects received 28 percent more money compared to non-Purpose requests. Loans were made at an even higher rate when those requesting them were perceived as trustworthy. The neural data showed that requests with transcendent purpose produced a larger oxytocin response than those without it.[40]

In another test, we ran a field experiment at a manufacturing business in the U.S. Midwest where we asked around 100 employees to perform work-related tasks while we monitored signals from their brains. Colleagues in the top quartile of alignment with the company's Purpose were 14 percent more productive than those in the bottom quartile, a statistically significant difference.[41]

In a third test, we examined the relationship between trust and Purpose by surveying a nationally representative sample of 1,095 working people in the United States (more details on this study are in chapter 11). Survey questions measured the eight OXYTOCIN factors, trust in one's colleagues, and the extent to which people thought their company had a transcendent purpose. We correlated the product trust × Purpose with answers to the question, "How much do you enjoy your job on a typical day?," on a 1-to-5 scale that measured Joy. We found a highly significant positive correlation between trust × Purpose and Joy of 0.77.[42]

The three studies, all using different methodologies, confirm that Purpose and trust produce Joy and provide some evidence that high-Purpose organizations have improved business outcomes.

Corroborating evidence. My results showing that Purpose improves performance have been corroborated by other researchers using different analytical approaches. Professor Raj Sisodia of Babson College selected public companies he identified as high Purpose and examined their stock prices. He found that stock returns of high-Purpose organizations outperformed the S&P 500 average by 8 to 1 from 1996 to 2006.[43] Jim Stengel, former global marketing officer of Procter & Gamble, used a different definition of Purpose and a different time period to analyze stock returns. He found that the return from holding the stocks of high-Purpose companies exceeded the S&P 500 average by 400 percent from 2001 to 2012.[44] Since stock returns reflect market participants' estimates of future profits, these analyses show that the millions of traders on the stock exchange are betting that Purpose improves performance. Establishing a transcendent purpose even improves performance of high school students doing "boring" tasks.[45]

Joy at Zappos. In our Zappos experiment, we asked one-half of the employees tested in groups of four to discuss Zappos's Purpose. The other half of Zapponians discussed, also in groups of four, a newspaper article about retail sales in their home city of Las Vegas. We took blood samples before and after these discussions, had participants complete surveys, and collected several streams of neurologic data throughout the discussion period and while participants did work-relevant tasks.

Our analysis showed that discussing Zappos's Purpose increased positive mood 10 percent from baseline (compared to a 3 percent reduction in positive mood for those discussing retail sales). Participants in the Purpose condition also had increased feelings of closeness to work colleagues by 16 percent (compared to a 7 percent reduction for those discussing retail sales). Perhaps most surprisingly, the Purpose group had a 44 percent smaller increase in heart rate from baseline to the discussion period compared to the retail sales group. Discussing Zappos's transcendent Purpose kept them markedly calmer. We found that when participants felt closer to their colleagues, their productivity was 15 percent higher in an objectively measureable task.

So what about culture fit? In addition to the neurologic data, we collected information on personality traits, including how agreeable and warm each person was. Using these data, we could decompose the proportion of their measured productivity that was due to "hiring the right people" (their personality) and due to discussing Zappos's Purpose. We found that 55 percent of productivity was attributed to hiring friendly, sociable people. The other 45 percent of work output was due to Purpose.[46]

This experiment shows that, at least at Zappos, culture is a powerful way to engage colleagues and increase productivity. Hiring matters, but so does culture. Hiring should assess the match of a candidate's own goals and Purpose with the organization's. If there is a Purpose match, the candidate is likely to be a highly engaged colleague, is more likely to stay with the organization long term, and is apt to accept a lower salary because of the implicit compensation of working for a high-Purpose company. Indeed, an experiment that randomly assigned participants to a good or poor Purpose match found that a Purpose fit increased productivity by 72 percent compared to poor matches.[47] Putting the right people in a high-trust culture and endowing it with Purpose produces the highest performance. As Steve Jobs said, "The only way to do great work is to love what you do."[48]

Why do Danes have so much Joy at work? Copenhagen's Happiness Research Institute surveyed 2,600 Danish employees to find out. Purpose was the clear winner, being twice as important as the second-rated factor (a great manager).[49] Additional Joy creators in Denmark are reasonable work hours (eXpectation), flat organizational structures (Transfer) where leaders ask for help rather than demand work be done (Natural), government-mandated life-long learning (Invest), and five to six weeks of vacation a year (Caring). Having spent time in Denmark, I can tell you that Danes are not just saying they have Joy at work—they show it.

☕ MONDAY MORNING LIST

▸ Measure Joy at work as a snapshot of how well your culture functions.

▸ Ask your most Joyful colleagues what makes them happy and create more of these opportunities.

▸ Use the founders' story to create a Purpose narrative.

▸ Collect Purpose narratives from colleagues and share these throughout the company.

▸ Create opportunities for colleagues to act on the organization's Purpose.

Chapter 11

Performance

Colleagues in the top quartile of trust are 50 percent more productive and have 106 percent more energy at work than those in the lowest trust quartile.

Walking to my meeting through an empty building filled with cobwebs was all the information I needed. This western United States consulting company had gone from being the premier place to work in its region to yesterday's news. The 2008 recession had hit it hard, but the trouble had begun a decade before, after its visionary founder passed away. Exiting the elevator on the third floor in the building where I would meet the new president and his senior staff, I saw a 1980s throwback wall-to-wall cube farm. Before ducking into the meeting room, I walked by a door with a sign that said "Executive Kitchen" and asked if I could get a cup of tea. A curled piece of paper taped below the sign warned "Executives and Their Assistants Only!"

The data I had collected before our meeting was grim. Trust was anemic, Purpose was vague, and Invest was nonexistent. The previous president had trimmed product lines, cut fat from budgets, and acquired a complementary company, but growth was tepid. The new president was a transformational leader, and I was going to help his team do a culture reboot.

It is infeasible to take blood and measure brain activity at most workplaces, so I developed a survey that would measure the OXYTOCIN factors as well as Purpose and Joy at work. It is called Ofactor. This is the survey you were asked to apply to your organization in chapter 1. Organizations use the insights from the Ofactor survey to run management experiments in order to improve business performance measures. Key outcomes that leaders seek to influence by changing culture include self-reported measures like energy at work and productivity, and objective measures such as profits, sick days, and colleague retention.

The Ofactor survey was developed using the science of the eight OXYTOCIN factors discussed in this book. Its predictive ability to capture the neurophysiologic markers of trust was confirmed in studies done in my laboratory and at two for-profit organizations that had colleagues complete the Ofactor survey and allowed us to collect neurologic data (including oxytocin measured in blood as well as electrocardiograms and skin conductance responses) while people worked. These field experiments also allowed us to objectively measure productivity and creative problem solving using incentivized and time-constrained tasks and correlate these with self-report measures.

Once we established the validity of the Ofactor survey, my group made it available to organizations to quantify and improve their cultures. I have been invited to work with companies and nonprofits in the United States, Europe, and Asia across a variety of industries, and in this chapter I share aggregated data from the approximately 5,000 colleagues whose companies have asked them to take the Ofactor survey. I also present the results from a representative sample of U.S. working adults who completed the survey.

I conducted this survey to rule out possible bias in data collected from companies that have asked for my help to improve their cultures. You will see that the national survey's findings are similar, though not identical, to the companies that have run management experiments based on their Ofactor results. This chapter concludes with your final Monday Morning List.

First, let's establish benchmarks. The Ofactor survey is designed so that the OXYTOCIN components and the Ofactor measure of organizational trust ("Ofactor") range from 0 to 100. No company has hit 100 for any of the factors, so seeking to reach 100 at your organization is unrealistic. Based on the national survey, organizations have high-trust cultures if their Ofactor score is above the 80th percentile. Trust is very high when Ofactor reaches or exceeds the 89th percentile.

Comparing data across all the companies that have used the Ofactor survey for culture interventions, one had the highest value for organizational trust. This is an extraordinarily well-run and profitable company. Slightly over 1,000 colleagues of this company took the Ofactor survey. Their average trust score was 88.05. The OXYTOCIN factors in this company varied from 84.11 (Openness) to 92.32 (Natural). These values may be near the highest attainable for an organization.

Each OXYTOCIN factor contributes linearly to the overall trust score, so a few low values for the OXYTOCIN components drive down trust. That is, high trust cultures have high values for all, or virtually all, of the OXYTOCIN factors. The values in the survey indicate which of the OXYTOCIN factors leaders should seek to improve by running management experiments. Like most effects in biology and economics, as an OXYTOCIN factor approaches its maximum value, the impact on performance diminishes. For this reason, the first management experiments most companies carry out are designed to raise the lowest OXYTOCIN components. This is a sensible approach, and I recommend you do likewise based on the data from your organization.

Management experiments are about doing, not simply measuring. This chapter relates Ofactor values to a variety of performance measures in order to convince you to start doing interventions in your organization.

For-profit companies. Several interesting findings emerge when aggregating data from companies that have taken the Ofactor survey as part of my work with them. The average Ofactor score is 73.17, a low value that shows these companies need to improve their cultures. The standard deviation (a measure of dispersion) in these data is 14.03. This means that there are some strong cultures in companies or divisions of companies, and that there are other places with very weak cultures. Organizations with very weak cultures are those with an Ofactor score of 59 or lower. Looking at data from individual colleagues, their judgments of trust in their organizations vary from 11 to 100.

The OXYTOCIN components also vary substantially. As mentioned in chapter 8, Invest is the lowest factor at most companies with which I have worked. The data corroborate my experience, with Invest having the lowest average value, 62.54, among the eight factors. The second-lowest factor is eXpectation, at 64.46. The factor with the highest average value is Natural, coming in at 82.42. Because it is an organization's leaders who request my help to improve their cultures, the average value for Natural may be biased upward. That is, Natural leaders may be more likely than other leaders to choose to use the Ofactor survey to improve their cultures. The average value of Natural in the national Ofactor survey is 70.33, confirming that leaders who have used the Ofactor survey score high on Natural. Across the OXYTOCIN factors, the average standard deviation is also large, exceeding 18. Again, this means that some organizations have built very strong aspects of culture, while many others are struggling to keep all the OXYTOCIN factors high.

This data set lets us examine how a culture of trust affects colleague engagement. First, we examined chronic stress. The correlation between trust and chronic stress was negative and nearly perfect, coming in at −0.93. This confirms the laboratory finding that chronic stress is a trust buster or, equivalently, that a culture of trust buffers stress. To understand why, we looked at the differences between colleagues who reported that their organizations are in the highest quartile of trust (average 90.94) and the lowest quartile of trust (average 51.98). Colleagues working in high-trust cultures experience 74 percent less chronic stress, have 36 percent more Joy at work, and are 28 percent more aligned with their organizations' Purpose. These findings show how a culture of trust motivates colleagues.

As mentioned above, my team ran a nationally representative Ofactor survey to confirm the findings from the select group of companies that had engaged me as a consultant. Data were collected by the survey firm Qualtrics in February 2016 from 1,095 people who were working full- or part-time. The data collection matched U.S. demographics, geographic density, and job types. Respondents also answered questions about their homes, health, and happiness. In this section, we focus on the 869 respondents working in for-profit businesses.

Each of the OXYTOCIN components showed a strong and positive statistical association with organizational trust. Overall, organizational trust was 70.24, just a bit lower than the sample of companies that had used the Ofactor survey to quantify their cultures. The highest factor was eXpectation, at 72.57, and the lowest was Ovation, at 66.71. As with the company data above, Invest was also low, coming in at 70.63. On a first pass, these data show that the average U.S. company could improve its cultures and boost performance by creating more Ovation and developing programs to Invest in colleagues. While your company may vary from the average, you should initially focus on these two factors.

The national survey, similar to the consulting survey, shows a high dispersion in organizational trust. Forty-seven percent of employees in the United States work in companies where organizational trust is below average, getting as abysmally low as 15. On the upside, 17 percent of employees work in very high-trust companies, with trust scores of 89 or above. This is good news. Very high-trust companies tend to be smaller, having an average of 222 colleagues, compared to an average of 333 for the entire sample. These companies are most often found in the Southern United States (from Texas to Florida) and have an overrepresentation of colleagues working in professional or technical fields.

The effect of trust on colleague motivation in the national sample was similar to what we found in the consulting sample. Colleagues who work for companies in the top quartile of trust (Ofactor score of 85 to 100) compared to those who work in the bottom quartile (Ofactor score of 15 to 58), are 50 percent more productive, have 106 percent more energy, and are 76 percent more engaged at work. Fifty percent more people who work in high-trust companies plan to stay with their employer over the next year, and 88 percent would recommend their company as a place to work to family and friends. Overall, employees in high-trust companies are 56 percent more satisfied with their jobs.

Those working in high-trust companies also experience 60 percent more Joy at work, align with their companies' Purpose 70 percent more, and feel 66 percent closer to their colleagues than people working in low-trust businesses. A high-trust culture even improves how people treat each other. Those in high-trust businesses have 11 percent more empathy for others, depersonalize colleagues

41 percent less, and face 40 percent less burnout from their work. Trust also improves colleagues' sense of accomplishment: In high-trust companies, personal achievement is 41 percent higher than in low-trust companies.

Our analysis revealed that these performance gains allow high-trust companies to pay their employees more. Colleagues earn an additional $6,450 a year, or 17 percent, working for companies in the highest quartile of trust, compared to colleagues in the lowest quartile. The only way high-trust companies can pay colleagues a higher salary in a competitive labor market is if they are more productive than those working in lower trust organizations. This is powerful evidence that trust directly improves profits.

Both sets of data from colleagues in the for-profit sector show that culture matters, improving the work lives of individuals and improving the bottom line for organizations.

Nonprofits. Does trust matter in nonprofits? Nonprofits have volunteer-employees and true volunteers, so one would think that culture would be even more important than in for-profits where pay may assuage distrust. But in my experience, few nonprofits take culture seriously enough to manage it. Another difficulty facing nonprofits is that the metrics for success are often less clear than they are for businesses: Does success mean the number of clients served? Grants funded? Donations? It may be all of these, or none.

Leaders of 29 nonprofits in the United States, Canada, Europe, and Asia asked their colleagues to take the Ofactor survey as part of a program I led to help these organizations understand and improve their cultures. A total of 278 employees and volunteers provided data. Ofactor scores across institutions ranged from 49 to 95; the Ofactor value for one respondent was dismal, at 11. The average value was 68.79. The lowest Ofactor component was Invest, at 58.35. This squares with what nonprofit executives have told me: They spend little on staff training and development. Caring and eXpectation were also quite low.

The data show that a culture of trust affects performance by volunteers and employees. As with for-profits, trust reduced chronic stress, again showing a nearly perfect negative correlation (–0.96). As with businesses, a culture of trust in nonprofits also increased engagement by colleagues using multiple measures. Comparing respondents in the highest quartile of trust to those in the lowest quartile (average Ofactor score of 92.03 versus 40.41), those in high-trust cultures had 109 percent more energy, were 64 percent more engaged, were 24 percent more productive, showed 39 percent more Joy at work, took 17 percent fewer sick days, and had 86 percent less chronic stress.

Let's check these results against the nationally representative Ofactor survey that included 122 people working at nonprofits. Average trust levels were 72.71, exceeding both the nonprofit sample from the group I led and the national for-profit average. Interestingly, the variation in trust among nonprofits is 19 percent lower than in businesses, showing that most nonprofits have fairly good cultures. In this sample of nonprofits, the highest factor was Transfer, with a value of 75.36, and the lowest, just like in the for-profit data, was Ovation, at 68.82. Invest was moderate, coming in at 74.0. The low Ovation is particularly surprising because recognizing colleagues can be done at no cost. As with the for-profit data, a culture of trust strongly correlated with outcomes nonprofits care about, including higher Joy and increased alignment with the organization's Purpose. In fact, compared to for-profit businesses, colleagues working at nonprofits in the sample had 5 percent more Joy and 10 percent more Purpose. Trust also increased colleague energy, productivity, retention, and engagement.

This analysis shows that culture at nonprofits is, on average, better than in businesses, and self-management is a key component that builds trust in social sector organizations. The data show that part of the culture advantage of nonprofits is the combination of high trust with high Purpose. As predicted by neuroscience studies, this produces more Joy for nonprofit colleagues than is experienced by those in business. This is intriguing because respondents in the nonprofit sector earn 12 percent less income on average than those who work for businesses ($36,950 versus $41,900). Colleagues in nonprofits appear to give up income to work in a culture that trusts them and has a transcendent purpose. Businesses that want to create engaging cultures should emulate what nonprofits are doing.

Government. The national Ofactor survey included 105 individuals working in local, state, or federal government agencies. The sample size is small, so the findings should not be considered fully reliable, but the trends are unlikely to surprise you. While trust was higher in nonprofits than in for-profit businesses, average organizational trust for government colleagues was low, 67.43. The averages of each of the OXYTOCIN components for government were below the average business values, with the lowest being Ovation (63.14), followed by Caring (67.29), and Invest (67.43). The only favorable finding for government is that Purpose exceeded that in business, coming in at 76.29, though this was still less than Purpose in nonprofits. Across all three sectors, Joy among colleagues was lowest for government, averaging 75.43.

Mirroring the frail culture reported by government colleagues, performance measures across the board were below those in businesses. These differences were not statistically different, because of the small sample of government colleagues, but the trends show what is happening. These data indicate that there is an endemic problem with the culture in government. The analysis predicts that performance by government agencies would improve if the culture were reformed.

Neurophysiologic experiments at businesses. The field experiment we ran at Zappos, mentioned in chapter 10, generated insights into how trust affects work performance and informs the findings from the Ofactor survey. We discovered that working with colleagues is stressful but that culture buffers stress. Zappos colleagues who discussed their culture, compared to the control group who discussed retail sales, had half the increase in heart rate from baseline when they were working with others. Measuring the fast-acting stress hormone adrenocorticotropin (ACTH) in blood confirmed this finding, falling 9 percent when Zapponians discussed their culture. At the same time, oxytocin increased over 18 percent in the culture group. These neurophysiologic changes when discussing Zappos's culture were associated with a 10 percent spike in happiness and a 16 percent increase in feelings of closeness to other Zapponians compared to the retail sales discussion group. And their Ofactor score? Respectable at 78. Discussing culture connected employees to each other and kept stress low.

The culture prime in the Zappos experiment directly increased productivity in a task we designed so it could be objectively measured. The increases in mood and closeness were statistically associated with higher productivity. Those in the highest quartile of positive mood were 29 percent more productive compared to those in the lowest quartile. Similarly, colleagues who felt closest to others were 49 percent more productive than those in the lowest quartile of closeness.

We dug a bit further to understand what made Zappos's culture so powerful by asking more than 1,000 Zapponians who were not in the experiment to take the Ofactor survey. All the OXYTOCIN components were high, exceeding 84, and trust came in at nearly 86. Fully 74 percent of the colleagues surveyed said they would not change a thing in Zappos's culture. One aspect that distinguishes Zappos's culture is that nearly every participant reported socializing with colleagues at work and after work. Participants in our experiment who socialized the most had one-third the cardiovascular stress after work tasks ended compared to those who socialized the least. Zappos has play rooms, hammocks, and other places where colleagues can take a break and hang out with their associates. This is not a waste of time but an effective way to recharge one's neural batteries and build social ties as we discussed in earlier chapters.[1]

The neurophysiological data show why culture affects engagement, health, and happiness. For example, Zapponians in the highest quartile of Joy took only three sick days in the last year compared to an average of seven. By affecting mood, productivity, and health, a culture of trust directly impacts an organization's bottom line.

My group also collected neurophysiologic measures and Ofactor data from 112 colleagues at a U.S. consumer services company.[2] Unlike in the Zappos study, we did not make culture salient by having colleagues discuss the company's Purpose. Instead, we collected neurophysiologic data with wireless sensors and blood draws while people worked. This approach was designed to capture the latent effect of culture due to variations across departments in the company and to relate these to engagement measures.

The company's overall trust score was on the low side, at 64.17. As with Zappos, we found that colleagues who reported higher levels of trust had statistically significantly more Joy, were more likely to agree with the organization's Purpose, had more energy at work, and said they were more productive. Trust also increased closeness to colleagues and substantially reduced chronic stress. Productivity was 21 percent higher for colleagues in this company who reported trust in the organization to be in the highest quartile compared to those in the lowest quartile of trust.

The physiologic data we collected helped explain these results. Overall, oxytocin increased 9 percent after people worked in groups of four, while stress hormones fell 3 percent. The variation from the lowest to the highest quartile of trust within this company is compelling. Colleagues in the highest trust quartile had a 228 percent larger increase in oxytocin compared to those in the lowest quartile. Those in the highest quartile also had much faster recovery from the stress of work, including a 155 percent faster drop in heart rate and a 221 percent larger decrease in the stress marker ACTH after work ended compared to those in the lowest quartile of trust. This shows again that culture affects our physiology, which in turn affects social behavior and productivity.

As discussed in chapter 10, culture should not be designed to make colleagues happy. We tested how work affects Joy by having participants do cognitively taxing work alone for three minutes. They were told they would only be paid for their work if it was sufficiently accurate. We found that the better people performed on this task, the happier they became (correlation of 0.25). This was true even taking into account people's baseline happiness levels. It is the process of doing challenging work, not necessarily hiring happy people, that produces Joy at work. We also found that when colleagues had an increase in positive mood during work, they felt closer to their colleagues.[3] These two effects caused them to put more effort into the next task we gave them and made it more fun to do. We also found a linear relationship between how close people felt to their colleagues and the reduction in the stress marker ACTH after work ended. The brains of colleagues who felt close to others at work jettisoned the stress of work more effectively than their associates who were less connected to their workmates. These results confirm that a culture of trust has a substantial effect on colleague motivation and results in more Joy while working.

Innovation. We designed a study for a midwestern U.S. manufacturing company to investigate how culture affects the ability to innovate. We did this by asking groups of four employees to solve an unusual problem. We instructed participants to assemble a mechanical apple peeler with 17 parts.[4] This is an odd device and is simple enough that people can put it together with moderate effort. We provided pictures of the completed device and gave groups of participants three minutes to assemble as many parts correctly as they could. The number of parts they put together allowed us to quantify how well teams could creatively problem-solve.

We found that the impact of culture on innovation was indirect. Those reporting high trust at work felt closer to work colleagues. In turn, those who were in the highest quartile of closeness to colleagues assembled 13.10 percent more apple-peeler parts than those lowest in closeness. Colleagues who felt close to each other also enjoyed finding solutions in this task 10 percent more than those in the bottom quartile of closeness. The causation matches the neurophysiologic findings in our other experiments: A high-trust culture increases closeness to colleagues, and when colleagues are closer to each other, they work together more effectively. These findings are consistent with a PricewaterhouseCoopers study showing that companies with high interpersonal trust are more innovative.[5] Trust and Joy even predict colleague creativity a year in the future, showing that culture has a lasting effect.[6]

Flourishing. At least 120,000 people die each year in the United States because of the chronic stress of work. The costs of stress-related illness and death are estimated to be up to $190 billion a year. Colleagues whose work is so burdensome that it inhibits their ability to meet family obligations are 90 percent more likely to suffer from ill health than those who have a reasonable work-life integration. The most important work-related influence on mortality risk is "low job control"—in other words, low trust.[7] Diminished physical and psychological health also reduce productivity and motivate colleagues to find another job.

We tested if high-trust, high-Purpose organizational cultures improve one's life outside of work by asking study participants a variety of questions about their personal lives. For the field experiment at the midwestern manufacturing company, we discovered that those in the highest quartile of trust were 12 percent more satisfied overall with their lives outside of work than those who were in the bottom quartile of trust. The next step was to figure out why.[8]

We found that trust decreases several measures of chronic stress. Those in the highest quartile of trust, compared to those in the lowest quartile, had baseline stress hormones that were 8.3 percent lower breathed 2.8 percent slower, and their hearts returned to baseline activity after work ended 9.3 percent faster. Another indicator of flourishing is that high-trust colleagues weigh 9.3 percent less than their lower-trust brethren (169.3 pounds compared to 185.1 pounds). These colleagues are also measurably healthier, taking 40 percent fewer sick days than less-trusted team members. This study provides several clues as to how trust at work produces health and happiness at home.

While these results made sense, they were only from a single company, so they might not generalize. In our nationally representative trust survey, we included additional measures of life satisfaction to see if the results held up. They did. Comparing those whose work cultures are in the highest quartile of trust to those in the lowest quartile, we found that high-trust colleagues' health was 13 percent better, they were 40 percent less likely to face burnout because of their work, and they were 41 percent less likely to depersonalize those at work—a sign of high chronic stress. Working in a high-trust culture was associated with 42 percent more energy at work and increased dedication at work by 55 percent. These data show that trust increases personal fulfillment at work and improves interpersonal behaviors.

We also found that working in a high-trust culture increased one's overall satisfaction with life by 29 percent. This could be due to two things our analysis uncovered. First, people who work in high-trust organizations show 11 percent more empathy for others, allowing them to build stronger emotional connections with the people around them. Second, those who work in high-trust organizations feel 38 percent closer to "something bigger than themselves." We included this spirituality question to test if the Invest component of trust would give people an opportunity to embrace a sense of meaning for their lives. These data suggest that it does. Organizational culture seeps into colleagues' personal lives—it is nearly impossible for it not to.

Return on culture. The payoffs to a high-trust culture include increased productivity, lower turnover, and lower chronic stress resulting in fewer sick days. Ill workers alone are estimated to account for 18 to 60 percent of workforce productivity losses so the effect of culture on profitability can be substantial.[9]

Using our nationally representative Ofactor data, we calculated the return on improving an organization's culture. A set of interventions that moved an organization up one quartile in trust would increase productivity by 25 percent, increase retention by 27 percent, and decrease the number of sick days by two per year per colleague. The average person in our data earns $40,550 a year. Assuming a colleague's productivity is two-thirds of that person's income, this culture change would increase the organization's output by $6,762 per person. Higher retention saves recruiting and training costs that vary widely by the type of job one does but are estimated to be an average of a year's salary for professional workers. The U.S. employee turnover rate is 15.1 percent annually. Assuming this holds at a typical business, a movement to a higher trust quartile would drop this to 11 percent. At the average salary in our data, this would produce a savings of $1,653 a year per colleague. Finally, we tallied the cost savings from the reduction in sick days. The United States is estimated to lose $576 billion a year from workplace sickness.[10] The costs are so high because being ill reduces productivity (39 percent of costs), increases costs for temp workers and workers' compensation (20 percent), and generates medical expenses (40 percent). Medical insurance in the United States in 2015 averaged $17,545 per employee, which, for this calculation, I assume declines when colleagues are healthier.[11] The other two costs—from reduced productivity and the expenses of temp workers and workers' compensation—can be estimated from the data in this paragraph. Using all three sources of savings, the reduction in medical costs would be $1,770 per colleague per year.[12] Adding up the value of the increases in productivity and retention, and the reduction in sick days, the total additional revenue each colleague would produce after moving up one quartile in trust would be $10,185.

For an organization with, for example, 500 colleagues, moving up one quartile on trust would increase revenue by $5.09 million every year. Assuming that the change in culture lasts 10 years, the present value of the additional cash flow from the investment in culture would be $26.5 million.[13] Using a typical hurdle rate on investments of 12 percent per year, a company should be willing to spend up to $8.5 million to improve its culture. The considerable return on a change in culture gives a company's leaders substantial scope to run management experiments that boost trust.

Other research groups confirm these findings. The Hay Group reports that highly engaged employees provide 89 percent greater customer satisfaction and fourfold higher revenue growth compared to disengaged employees.[14] Another research study found that organizations with higher than average employee engagement had, compared to average companies, customer loyalty that was 50 percent higher and profits that were 27 percent higher.[15]

The higher revenue at companies with great cultures is reflected in analyses by Alex Edmans of the University of Pennsylvania's Wharton School. He found that stock market returns for companies in *Fortune* magazine's 100 Best Companies to Work For list exceeded their peers by 73.5 percent from 1984 to 2005.[16] Companies with better cultures are more productive and, as a result, the value of their revenue eclipses their peers', driving up stock valuations.

Before and after culture change. The consulting company with the cobweb-filled building that opened this chapter developed a plan to transform its culture, empower colleagues, and jump-start growth. One of its executives told me before I started my work there that he thought all this "touchy-feely stuff was hooey." This is where knowing the science of voluntary cooperation and having the data to back it up comes in. I spent two days going through this company's Ofactor data and providing examples of companies that have created high-trust cultures in order to spark ideas in the executive team. The question was, of course, where to start.

Changes had to be made immediately to signal that positive improvements were afoot. I mentioned that the taped-up paper sign on the executive kitchen door saying "Executives and Their Assistants Only!" sent entirely the wrong message about teamwork. The president of the company said, "I have worked here a year, and every day that sign bothers me." "Bill," I said, "you are the president. Tear down that sign." Bill marched out of the room and returned with the sign in his hands. The entire room cheered as he tore it to pieces and threw them into the air.

By the end of the second day, I had helped the executive team clarify their goals and identify management experiments to run. Two months later, Bill held a town hall meeting to explain the changes being made and why they would benefit everyone working there. The cube farm was being phased out for an open-office plan, training and conference attendance were reinstated, and the organization's strategic plan would be shared with everyone. The chief learning officer trained supervisors to be coaches and taught them to set clear eXpectations. Daily huddles were added to ensure progress toward goals was being made. In one of the most sweeping changes, the annual review was scrapped for a forward-looking Whole Person Review. Staff and supervisors were thrilled. The leadership team was fully on board with the culture change. All, that is, except Mr. It's Hooey. Once the changes started having an effect, the president politely told him it was time to look for new employment.

Let's look at this organization's data to quantify the impact of its management experiments one year after collecting baseline data. The management experiments the executive team implemented took time to execute, so the data here represent only about six months of impact. A total of 1,841 colleagues completed the two waves of the Ofactor survey. Organizational trust before the management experiments started was 74.68. A year later, trust had increased to 78.98. Every one of the individual OXYTOCIN factors increased, with changes between 3.3 and 9.1 percent. The largest increases were in eXpectation (9.1 percent) and Invest (7.1 percent), both factors that had been quite low at baseline. The data also showed that Purpose increased 7 percent, Joy 7.3 percent, and dreading being at work fell over 14 percent. The culture improvements produced an increase in energy at work of 11.1 percent, a self-reported productivity increase of 4.3 percent, and nearly 8 percent higher engagement. Each of the reported changes from year one to year two was statistically greater than zero.

The triple bottom line. Culture matters. A culture of trust and Purpose resonates with the social nature of human beings and creates engagement, Joy, and profits. This book has shown how building a high-trust culture drives the triple bottom line: It is good for colleagues, good for the organization, and good for society. I hope you will consider your organization's culture as the strategic asset that it is. Like any asset, it must be monitored and managed. If you do not manage your culture, it will surely manage you.

Neuromanagement provides a framework to understand why volunteer-employees continue to show up; spend their energy moving the organization's goals forward; and, at best, occasionally send 3 a.m. emails. Neuroscience belongs in the board room, on the factory floor, and in store aisles. When organizations embrace their core humanity, they treat everyone at work like human beings rather than human resources. It's not rocket science, but it is neuroscience. And it is smart business.

☕ MONDAY MORNING LIST

▶ Using the Ofactor data you collected, identify the lowest OXYTOCIN component.

▶ Identify business outcomes that your lowest OXYTOCIN factor may be affecting and measure them.

▶ Design a management experiment to change your lowest OXYTOCIN factor and specify the period of the change.

▶ Communicate to your colleagues the change you will make and the reason for it.

▶ After the experiment period, remeasure the OXYTOCIN factors and the key outcomes you sought to affect.

▶ Repeat using other OXYTOCIN factors.

Acknowledgments

I am grateful to my wife and children for support and forbearance while I wrote this book, innumerable graduate students and faculty in my lab for running countless experiments to explore the neuroscience of organizational trust, and graduate students at Claremont Graduate University who took my classes and helped me understand what I was really doing. Special thanks to Ken Nowack and Andy Parkinson who prodded me to go from creating a research tool to stepping in to improve organizations.

Notes

INTRODUCTION

1   J. Henrich, "Culture and Social Behavior," *Current Opinion in Behavioral Sciences* 3 (2015): 84–89.

2   P. J. Zak, "Building Trust Is a Blood Sport," *Ivey Business Journal.* November/December 2015.

3   Danny Miller and Jon Hartwick, "Spotting Management Fads," *Harvard Business Review,* October 2002.

4   P. J. Zak and S. Knack. "Trust and Growth," *The Economic Journal,* 111 (2001): 295–321.

5   S. Knack and P. J. Zak, "Building Trust: Public Policy, Interpersonal Trust, and Economic Development," *Supreme Court Economic Review* 10 (2002): 91–107.

6   P.J. Zak. The Science Behind Building a Culture of Trust. *TD Magazine,* June 2016: 48–53.

7   James K. Harter, Frank L. Schmidt, and Theodore L. Hayes, "Business-Unit-Level Relationship Between Employee Satisfaction, Employee Engagement, and Business Outcomes: A Meta-analysis." *Journal of Applied Psychology* 87, no. 2 (2002): 268.

8   Laszlo Bock, *Work Rules! Insights from Inside Google That Will Transform How You Live and Lead* (New York: Twelve, 2015).

9   Accenture, "7 Ways Federal Agencies Can Reduce Cost and Improve Workforce Productivity," https://www.accenture.com/us-en/insight-seven-ways-reduce-costs-improve-workforce-productivity-summary.aspx.

10 Bourree Lam, "Why Do Workers Feel So Unhappy? Just One-Fifth

of Employees Report Believing That Their Workplaces Strongly Value Them," *Atlantic,* November 4, 2014.

11 "Employee Job Satisfaction and Engagement: Optimizing Organizational Culture for Success," SHRM, 2015. https://www.shrm.org/hr-today/trends-and-forecasting/research-and-surveys/pages/job-satisfaction-and-engagement-report-optimizing-organizational-culture-for-success.aspx.

12 http://www.nytimes.com/2016/02/28/magazine/what-google-learned-from-its-quest-to-build-the-perfect-team.html?_r=1.

13 PricewaterhouseCoopers, 18th Annual Global CEO Survey, http://www.pwc.com/gx/en/ceo-agenda/ceosurvey/2015.html.

14 "4 Ways Businesses Can Build Customer Trust," World Economic Forum, https://www.weforum.org/agenda/2016/01/4-ways-business-can-build-trust/http://www3.weforum.org/docs/WEFEvolution Trust BusinessDeliveryValues_report_2015.pdf.

15 John F. Helliwell, and Haifang Huang, "Well-Being and Trust in the Workplace," *Journal of Happiness Studies* 12 no. 5 (2011): 747-767.

16 Boston Consulting Group, "Global Workforce Crisis Puts $10 Trillion at Risk in World Economy, Study Says," press release, December 11, 2014.

17 Maurer, Roy, *Skills Gap, Turnover Are Top Talent Concerns, 2015,* Society for Human Resource Management, https://www.shrm.org/resourcesandtools/hr-topics/talent-acquisition/pages/skills-gap-turnover-talent-concerns.aspx.

18 Anne Bahr Thompson, "The Intangible Things Employees Want from Employers," *Harvard Business Review,* December 3, 2015.

19 Bill George with Peter Sims, *True North: Discover Your Authentic Leadership* (New York: Jossey-Bass, 2007.

20 For example, Alan E. Hall, *The 7 C's of Hiring* (Seattle: Amazon Digital Services, 2012); Bock, *Work Rules!;* Martin Yate, *Knock 'em Dead Hiring the Best: Proven Tactics for Successful Employee Selection* (New York: Adams Media, 2014).

21 Issie Lapowsky, "Zappos Goes Flat, Gets Rid of Managers," December 30, 2013, http://www.inc.com/issie-lapowsky/zappos-gets-rid-of-managers.html?cid=readmore.

22 V. Alexander and P. J. Zak, *Office Design Affects Creative Problem Solving: A Neuroscience Study* (in review).

23 Edward G. Mahon, Scott N. Taylor, and Richard E. Boyatzis, "Antecedents of Organizational Engagement: Exploring Vision, Mood and Perceived Organizational Support with Emotional Intelligence As a Moderator," *Frontiers in Psychology* (2014): doi:

10.3389/fpsyg.2014.01322; Liz Ryan, "The Employee Engagement Scam," (2014), LinkedIn, https://www.linkedin.com/pulse/ 2014092 6142036-52594-the-employee-engagement-scam; Laurie Bassi and Dan McMurrer, "Does Engagement Really Drive Results?," *Talent Management Magazine*, March 2010; P. M. Wright, T. M. Gardner, L. M. Moynihan, and M. R. Allen, "The Relationship Between HR Practices and Firm Performance: Examining Causal Order," *Personnel Psychology* 58, no. 2 (2005): 409–446.

24 Caroline Fairchild, "Workplace Happiness Survey Finds Friends Are More Important Than Salary," *Huffington Post*, October 23, 2012; J. A. Barraza and P. J. Zak, "Empathy Toward Strangers Triggers Oxytocin Release and Subsequent Generosity," *Annals of the New York Academy of Sciences* 1167 (2009): 182–189; J. A. Barraza, M. E. McCullough, S. Ahmadi, and P. J. Zak, "Oxytocin Infusion Increases Charitable Donations," *Hormones and Behavior* 60 (2011): 148–151.

25 http://www.druckerinstitute.com/2013/07/of-customers-and-comrades/.

CHAPTER 1

1 Nikita Lalwani, "In Trust We Trust," *Times* (London), June 2, 2012.

2 P. J. Zak, R. Kurzban, S. Ahmadi, et al, "Testosterone Administration Decreases Generosity in the Ultimatum Game," *PLOS ONE* 4, no. 12 (2009), http://dx.doi.org/10.1371/journal.pone.0008330.

3 This experiment was commissioned by the BBC and performed May 29, 2011.

4 P. J. Zak, *The Moral Molecule: The Source of Love and Prosperity* (New York: Dutton, 2012).

5 D. McGregor, *The Human Side of Enterprise*. New York: McGraw-Hill, 1960.

6 http://www.zanebenefits.com/blog/bid/312123/Employee-Retention-The-Real-Cost-of-Losing-an-Employee.

7 Frederick Winslow Taylor, (1911), *The Principles of Scientific Management*. New York and London: Harper & Brothers, 1911.

8 T. A. Judge, R. F. Piccolo, N. P. Podsakoff, J. C. Shaw, and B. L. Rich, "The Relationship Between Pay and Job Satisfaction: A Meta-analysis of the Literature," *Journal of Vocational Behavior*, 77 no. 2 (2010), 157–167.

9 Michael I. Norton, Daniel Mochon, and Dan Ariely. "The 'IKEA Effect': When Labor Leads to Love." *Harvard Business School*

Marketing Unit Working Paper 11-091 (2011); D. Pink, *Drive: The Surprising Truth About What Motivates Us.* New York: Riverhead Books, 2011.

10 Laszlo Bock, *Work Rules! Insights from Inside Google That Will Transform How You Live and Lead* (New York: Twelve, 2015).

CHAPTER 2

1 Note that the annual turnover rate for retail full-time employees is 27 percent. http://blogs.wsj.com/atwork/2015/02/19/one-reason-walmart-is-raising-pay-turnover/; http://www.businessinsider.com/walmart-target-and-tj-maxx-are-facing-a-worker-crisis-2015-10.

2 P. Godar, "Recognition: Are You Using This Powerful Tool to Connect People and Performance?," http://www.maritz.com/~/media/Files/MaritzDotCom/News%20Events%20and%20Insights/Maritz%20In%20The%20News/News-HRM-Recognition-Powerful-Tool.ashx.

3 http://www.octanner.com/blog/category/leadership.

4 http://intelispend.com/blog/23-employee-motivation-statistics-to-silence-naysayers/.

5 5/1/2011.

6 Naomi I. Eisenberger, Matthew D. Lieberman, and Kipling D. Williams, "Does Rejection Hurt? An fMRI Study of Social Exclusion." *Science* 302 no. 5643 (2003): 290–292.

7 "Adapting To The Realities of Our Changing Workforce," Workforce Mood Tracker, Spring 2014, http://go.globoforce.com/rs/globoforce/images/Spring2014MoodTrackerGloboforce.pdf.

8 Rainer Strack, Jean-Michel Caye, Thomas Gaissmaier, et al, "Creating People Advantage 2014–2015: How to Set Up Great HR Functions: Connect, Prioritize, Impact," December 1, 2014, https://www.bcgperspectives.com/content/articles/human_resources_creating_people_advantage_2014_how_to_set_up_great_hr_functions/.

9 Edward L. Deci, "Effects of Externally Mediated Rewards on Intrinsic Motivation." *Journal of personality and Social Psychology* 18 no. 1 (1971): 105; Edward L. Deci and Richard M. Ryan. "The general Causality Orientations Scale: Self-determination in Personality." *Journal of Research in Personality* 19 no. 2 (1985): 109–134; Andreas, Mojzisch and Stefan Schulz-Hardt, "Being Fed Up," *Annals of the New York Academy of Sciences* 1118 no. 1 (2007): 186–205.; D. Pink,

Drive: The Surprising Truth About What Motivates Us, New York: Riverhead Books, 2011.

10 Bob Chapman (Barry-Wehmiller CEO), interview with the author, April 25, 2013, St. Louis, MO.

11 Bob Chapman (Barry-Wehmiller CEO), interview with the author, April 23, 2013, St. Louis, MO.

12 http://www.trulyhumanleadership.com/?page_id=36.

CHAPTER 3

1 "43 percent of highly engaged employees get weekly feedback: The 2014 Global Workforce Study Driving Engagement Through a Consumer-Like Experience," TowersWatson, 2014. https://www.towerswatson.com/en-US/Insights/IC-Types/Survey-Research-Results/2014/08/the-2014-global-workforce-study.

2 Bill Turque. "Rhee: Election Result 'Devastating' for D.C. Schoolchildren". *Washington Post*, September 16, 2010, http://voices.washingtonpost.com/dcschools/2010/09/rhee election_result_devastati.html.

3 Sewell Chan, "The Highest Per-Pupil Spending in the U.S.," *New York Times*, May 24, 2007, http://empirezone.blogs.nytimes.com/2007/05/24/the-highest-per-pupil-spending-in-the-us/?_r=0.

4 "IMPACT: An Overview," District of Columbia, Public Schools 2014, http://dcpsdc.gov/page/impact-overview, http://articles washingtonpost.com/2009-10-01/news/36910694_1_teacher-performance-rhee-district-teachers; http:// www.documentcloud.org/documents/05699 incentives-selection-and-teacher-performance.html.

5 B. Turque, "Fenty's Political Fortunes Tied to Success of D.C. School Reforms," *Washington Post*, August 19, 2010.

6 http://usatoday30.usatoday.com/news/education/2011-03-28-1Aschooltesting28_CV_N.htm.

7 https://news.tn.gov/node/11644.

8 D. R. Forsyth, "Performance," in *Group Dynamics* (5th ed.), ed. D.R. Forsyth, (Belmont: CA, Wadsworth, Cengage Learning, 2006), 280–2309.

9 Alan G. Ingham, George Levinger, James Graves, and Vaughn Peckham, "The Ringelmann Effect: Studies of Group Size and Group Performance," *Journal of Experimental Social Psychology* 10, no. 4 (July 1974): 371–384.

10 Google People Dev group interview with the author, Mountain View, CA, February 25, 2015.

11 Meghan Busse, Jeroen Swinkels, and Greg Merkley, Enterprise Rent-A-Car, Kellogg School of Management Case KEL612, 2012. http://www.kellogg.northwestern.edu/kellogg-case-publishing/case-search/case-detail.aspx?caseid=%7BE966E1B9-061D-499C-B8FF-D248F003BD3A%7D.

12 "No. 5 Enterprise: A Clear Road to the Top," *Business Week,* September 18, 2006.

13 https://hbr.org/2011/06/defend-your-research-what-makes-a-team-smarter-more-women.

14 Teresa Amabile and Steven J. Kramer, "The Power of Small Wins," *Harvard Business Review,* May 2011, https://hbr.org/2011/05/the-power-of-small-wins/ar/1; Nicholas Christakis and James Fowler, *Connected: The Surprising Power of Our Social Networks and How They Shape Our Lives—How Your Friends' Friends' Friends Affect Everything You Feel, Think, and Do* (New York: Little, Brown, 2011).

15 Max Nisen, "Why GE Had to Kill Its Annual Performance Reviews After More Than Three Decades," August 13, 2015 http://qz.com/428813/ge-performance-review-strategy-shift/.

16 Dov Eden, "Leadership Expectations' Pygmalion Effect," *Leadership Quarterly,* 3 no. 4, 271–305 (1992). A. S. King, "Self-Fulfilling Prophecy in Training the Hard-Core: Supervisor Expectations and the Underprivileged Workers' Performance," *Social Science Quarterly,* 52 (1971); 369–378; A. S. King, "Expectation Effects in Organization Change," *Administrative Science Quarterly,* 19 (1974), 221–230.; D. Eden and A. B. Shani, "Pygmalion goes to boot camp: Expectancy, Leadership, and Trainee Performance," (1982). *Journal of Applied Psychology, 67,* 195–199.

17 C. A. O'Reilly, *New United Motors Manufacturing, Inc.*(NUMMI). Stanford Graduate School of Business (1998).

18 John Shook, "How to Change a Culture: Lessons from NUMMI," *MIT Sloan Management Review* (January 1, 2010).

19 http://www.epa.gov/lean/environment/studies/gm.htm.

20 "Fun and Games at Work," The Drucker Exchange, January 13, 2014, http://thedx.druckerinstitute.com/2014/01/fun-and-games-at-work/.

21 http://intelispend.com/blog/23-employee-motivation-statistics-to-silence-naysayers.

22 Ethan R. Mollick, and Nancy Rothbard, "Mandatory Fun: Consent,

Gamification and the Impact of Games at Work." *The Wharton School* research paper series (2014).

CHAPTER 4

1   Rachel Feintzeig, "Flexibility at Work: Worth Skipping a Raise?" October 31, 2014, http://blogs.wsj.com/atwork/2014/10/31/flexibility-at-work-worth-skipping-a-raise/.

2   Bob Chapman, interview, April 25, 2013.

3   Rick Wartzman, "The Difference Between Work-Life Integration and Workaholism," *Fortune*, February 18, 2015, http://fortune.com/2015/02/18/work-life-time-management/.

4   Kevin Freiberg, and Jackie Freiberg *Guts!: Companies that Blow the Doors off Business-as-Usual,* (New York: Doubleday, 2004), 80.

5   Dennis Campbell, Marc J. Epstein, and F. Asis Martinez-Jerez, "The Learning Effects of Monitoring," *Accounting Review 86, no. 6 (November 2011): 1909–1934.*

6   Erin Griffith, "*Amazon CEO Jeff Bezos: I've made billions of dollars of failures,*" *Fortune* http://fortune.com/2014/12/02/amazon-ceo-jeff-bezos-failure/.

7   Linda A. Hill, Greg Brandeau, Emily Truelove, and Kent Lineback, *Collective Genius: The Art and Practice of Leading Innovation* (Cambridge: Harvard Business Review Press, 2014).

8   C. Argyris and D. Schön, *Organizational Learning: A Theory of Action Perspective* (Reading, MA: Addison-Wesley, 1978).

9   C. Argyris, *Increasing Leadership Effectiveness* (New York: Wiley, 1976).

10 W. Bachman, "Nice Guys Finish First: A SYMLOG Analysis of U.S. Naval Commands," in *The SYMLOG Practitioner*, ed. R. B. Polley, A. P. Hare, and P. J. Stone, (New York: Praeger, 1988), 133–153.

11 Liz Riggs, "Why Do Teachers Quit?," *Atlantic*, October 18, 2013, http://www.theatlantic.com/education/archive/2013/10/why-do-teachers-quit/280699/.

12 Bruce D. Kirkcaldy, Roy J. Shephard, and Adrian F. Furnham, "The Influence of Type A Behaviour and Locus of Control Upon Job Satisfaction and Occupational Health," *Personality and Individual Differences* 33 (2002): 1361–1371.

13 Zappos colleague, communication to the author, June 28, 2016.

14 Michael R. Kukenberger, John E. Mathieu, and Thomas Ruddy, "A Cross-Level Test of Empowerment and Process Influences on

Members' Informal Learning and Team Commitment," *Journal of Management* (September 11, 2012): doi: 1177/0149206312443559.

15 Kamalini Ramdas and Ravindra Gajulapalli, HCL Technologies, "Employee First, Customer Second," Darden School Case UV1085. 2008.

16 Alan MacCormack, Fiona Murray, and Erika Wagner, "Spurring Innovation Through Competitions," *MIT Sloan* (Fall 2013).

17 General Stanley McChrystal, *My Share of the Task: A Memoir*. (New York: Penguin, 2013).

18 As quoted in: J. L. Elkhorne, Edison—The Fabulous Drone, in Amateur Radio 73 Vol. XLVI, No. 3 (March 1967): 52–56.

19 Seth Stevenson, "Don't Go to Work," *Slate*, May 11, 2014, http://www.slate.com/articles/business/psychology_of_management/2014/05/best_buy_s_rowe_experiment_can_results_only_work_environments_actually_be.html.

20 Ibid.

21 Monique Valcour, "The End of 'Results Only' at Best Buy Is Bad News," *Harvard Business Review*, March 8, 2013, http://blogs.hbr.org/2013/03/goodbye-to-flexible-work-at-be/; Thomas Lee, "Best Buy Ends Flexible Work Program for its Corporate Employees," Star Tribune, December 13, 2013, http://www.startribune.com/no-13-best-buy-ends-flexible-work-program-for-its-corporate-employees/195156871/.

22 Mary S. Logan and Daniel C. Ganster, "The Effects of Empowerment on Attitudes and Performance: The Role of Social Support and Empowerment Beliefs," *Journal of Management Studies* 44, no. 8 (2007): 1523–1550.

23 Conscious Capitalism 2014, April 10, San Diego, CA.

CHAPTER 5

1 Gary Hamel, "First, Let's Fire All the Managers." *Harvard Business Review* 89 no. 12 (2011): 48–60.

2 P.J. Zak, *The Moral Molecule: The Source of Love and Prosperity*. (New York: Dutton, 2012); Chris Rufer (Morning Star Company owner-founder), interview with the author, August 11, 2011, Los Banos, CA.

3 "What People Earn 2016," *Parade*, April 10, 2016, 6–9.

4 The HOW Report: A Global, Empirical Analysis of How Governance, Culture, and Leadership Impact Performance, 2015. LRN.

5   http://www.businesswire.com/news/home/20120215005284/en/
Intelligent-Office-Survey-Finds-People-Don't-Corporate#.
VWIW12DWvpj.

6   J. Reeve and C. M. Tseng, "Cortisol Reactivity to a Teacher's
Motivating Style: The Biology of Being Controlled Versus Supporting
Autonomy," *Motivation and Emotion*, 35 no. 1 (2011): 63–74; P.
Lindfors and U. Lundberg, "Is Low Cortisol Release an Indicator of
Positive Health?," *Stress and Health* 18, no. 4 (2002): 153–160.

7   James E. Maddux, ed. *Self-Efficacy, Adaptation, and Adjustment:
Theory, Research, and Application*, Plenum Series in Social/Clinical
Psychology (New York: Springer, 1995).

8   Carol D. Ryff and Corey Lee M. Keyes, "The Structure of
Psychological Well-Being Revisited." *Journal of Personality and Social
Psychology* 69 no. 4 (1995): 719.

9   C. Dormann, D. Fay, D. Zapf, and M. Frese, "A State-Trait Analysis
of Job Satisfaction: On the Effect of Core Self-Evaluations," *Applied
Psychology: An International Review* 55, no. 1 (2006): 27–51.

10   Mihaly Csikszentmihalyi, *Finding Flow* (New York: Basic Books,
1997).

11   *Valve Corporation Employee Handbook*, 2012, 9.

12   Ibid., 20.

13   Claire Suddath, "Why There Are No Bosses at Valve," *Bloomberg
Businessweek*, April 27, 2012. http://www.businessweek.com/articles/
2012-04-27/why-there-are-no-bosses-at-valve.

14   http://www.nucor.com/story/chapter4/.

15   Robert Heller, "Company Management the Nucor Way," *Management
Issues*, June 22, 2007 http://www.management-issues.com/opinion
/4292/company-management-the-nucor-way/.

16   Albert Bandura, "Moral Disengagement in the Perpetration of
Inhumanities," *Personality and Social Psychology Review* 3 no. 3 (1999):
193–209.

17   Bourree Lam, "Why Are So Many Zappos Employees Leaving?"
Atlantic, January 15, 2016, http://www.theatlantic.com/business/
archive/2016/01/zappos-holacracy-hierarchy/424173/.

18   http://www.washingtonpost.com/business/a-company-that-profits-
as-it-pampers-workers/2014/10/22/d3321b34-4818-11e4-b72e-
d60a9229cc10_story.html.

19   Ricardo Semler, "Managing Without Managers," *Harvard Business
Review* September–October 1989.

20   Bill McKinney of Strategy and Long Term Development at Thrivent

Financial, interview with the author, June 2013, Claremont, CA, and email confirmation, June 2015.

21 http://firstround.com/review/bureaucracy-isnt-inevitable-heres-how-airbnb-beat-it/.

22 G. Hamel, "First, let's fire all the managers," *Harvard Business Review*, 89 no. 12 (2011), 48–60.

23 A. D. Stajkovic and F. Luthans, "Self-Efficacy and Work-Related Performance: A Meta-Analysis," *Psychological Bulletin* 124, no. 2 (1998): 240–261.

24 Bradley L. Kirkman and Benson Rosen, "Beyond Self-Management: Antecedents and Consequences of Team Empowerment," *Academy of Management Journal* 42, no. 1 (February 1999): 58–74; G. P. Latham and C. A. Frayne, "Self-Management Training for Increasing Job Attendance: A Follow-Up and a Replication," *Journal of Applied Psychology* 74, no. 3 (1989): 411–416.

25 G. P. Latham, "The Motivational Benefits of Goal-Setting," *The Academy of Management Executive*, 18 no. 4 (2004), 126–129.

26 http://hbswk.hbs.edu/item/is-the-time-right-for-self-management.

27 S. S. Nandram, *Organizational Innovation by Integrating Simplification*. (Switzerland: Springer International Publishing, 2015), 135–162.

28 Karen Monsen, and Jos deBlok, *Buurtzorg Nederland American Journal of Nursing*, 113 no. 8 (2013): 55–.

29 David Marquet, "Why Motivating Others Starts with Using the Right Language," 99U, n.d.,http://99u.com/articles/25567/why-motivating-others-starts-with-using-the-right-language?

30 Michael Tsonis (lieutenant commander, U.S. Navy), conversation with the author, April 2, 2015, Claremont, CA. The opinions expressed do not represent those of the Strategic Studies Group or the U.S. Navy.

31 Alicia Ciccone, "Bad Bosses Cause Employee Stress, Poor Health," *Huffington Post*, August 6, 2012, http://www.huffingtonpost.com/2012/08/06/bad-bosses-employee-stress_n_1747565.html .

32 http://pages.lrn.com/how-report.

33 http://www.druckerinstitute.com/2013/12/its-not-you-its-me/.

34 A. Gostick, and C. Elton, *All In: How the Best Managers Create a Culture of Belief and Drive Big Results*. (New York: Simon and Schuster 2012).

35 Freek Vermeulen, "What Happens When All Employees Work When They Feel Like It," *Harvard Business Review*, December 17, 2014.

36 "Progress: Responding to Global Changes,"Global Citizenship

Report, http://www.citigroup.com/citi/about/data/corp_citizenship /2014-citi-global-citizenship-report-en.pdf.

37 Nicholas Bloom, James Liang, John Roberts, and Jenny Ying, "Does Working from Home Work? Evidence From a Chinese Experiment," (No. w18871). National Bureau of Economic Research, February 2013; American Psychological Association, "Telecommuting Has Mostly Positive Consequences for Employees and Employers, Say Researchers," press release, November 19, 2001, http://www.apa.org/ news/press/releases/2007/11/telecommuting.aspx.

38 http://www.pcworld.com/article/2038639/why-yahoos-tele commuting-ban-is-still-bad-for-business.html.

39 http://www.diw.de/documents/publikationen/73/diw_01.c.510143. de/diw_sp0768.pdf.

40 Andrea Tyler, "This Weird Management Style Turned Around My Small Business," *CBS Small Business Pulse*, October 19, 2015, http:// cbspulse.com/2015/10/19/indinero-success-unique-management-style/.

41 Alana Semuels, "The Happier Workplace, *Atlantic*, November 30, 2014, http://www.theatlantic.com/business/archive/2014/11/the -happier-workplace/383137/.

42 Veronika Alexander and Paul J. Zak, "How Open Office Design Affects Teamwork: A Neurophysiological Field Study," in review.

43 Tim Brown (CEO of IDEO), conversation with the author, San Francisco, August 19, 2015

44 http://www.fastcompany.stfi.re/3056662/the-future-of-work/she-created-netflixs-culture-and-it-ultimately-got-her-fired?sf=xpejke.

45 Steve Chawkins, "Andrew Kay dies at 95; inventor pioneered compact computers," *Los Angeles Times*, September 10, 2014.

46 https://hbr.org/2015/06/are-we-more-productive-when-we-have-more-time-off.

47 Y. Chouinard, *Let My People Go Surfing: The Education of a Reluctant Businessman.* (New York: Penguin, 2006).

CHAPTER 6

1 https://open.bufferapp.com/introducing-open-salaries-at-buffer-including-our-transparent-formula-and-all-individual-salaries/.

2 http://intelispend.com/blog/23-employee-motivation-statistics-to-silence-naysayers.

3 David A. Garvin, "How Google Sold Its Engineers on Management," *Harvard Business Review*, December 2013.

4 David A. Garvin, Alison Berkley Wagonfeld, and Liz Kind. "Google's Project Oxygen: Do Managers Matter." *HBSP Case study* (2013).

5 "State of the American Manager: Analytics and Advice for Leaders," http://www.gallup.com/services/182138/state-american-manager.aspx.

6 Justin Brady, "The Air Force General Who Channels a Mellow CEO's Leadership Style," *Washington Post*, May 14, 2014.

7 Michael E. Palanski, Surinder S. Kahai, and Francis J. Yammarino, "Team Virtues and Performance: An Examination of Transparency, Behavioral Integrity, and Trust," *Journal of Business Ethics*, 99 no. 2 (2011): 201–216, doi: 10.1007/s10551-010-0650-7.7.

8 Emiliano Huet-Vaughn, "The Unexpected Benefit of Telling People What Their Coworkers Make," *Atantic*, April 8, 2014.

9 Jerre Stead (former CEO of NCR Corp.), conversation with the author, Feb. 6, 2004, Claremont, CA.

10 http://blog.hubspot.com/blog/tabid/6307/bid/34234/The-HubSpot-Culture-Code-Creating-a-Company-We-Love.aspx.

11 Ethan Bernstein, "The Smart Way to Create a Transparent Workplace: Openness Can Raise Productivity—and Undermine It," *Wall Sreet Journal*, February 22, 2015.

12 Laszlo Bock, *Work Rules! Insights from Inside Google That Will Transform How You Live and Lead* (New York: Twelve, 2015).

13 HCL Technologies, "Employee First."

14 Clive Thompson, "The See-Through CEO," *Wired*, April 4, 2007, http://www.wired.com/2007/04/wired40-ceo/.

15 J. Choi, "How Radical Transparency Kills Stress," *Fast Company*, July 15, 2013, http://www.fastcompany.com/3014160/how-to-be-a-success- at-everything/how radical-transparency-kills-stress.

16 https://www.qualtrics.com/blog/radical-transparency-leads-high-employee-engagement/.

17 John Mackey (Whole Foods CEO), interview with the author, December 10, 2010, Lake Arrowhead, CA.

18 P. LeBarre, "Forget Empowerment—Aim for Exhilaration," Management Innovation eXchange, April 2012, http://www.managementexchange.com/blog/forget-empowerment-aim-exhilaration; R. Semler, "Managing Without Managers," *Harvard Business Review*, September-October, 1989.

19 http://www.des.wa.gov/SiteCollectionDocuments/About/Lean_culture/Lean_Culture_at_DES.pdf.

CHAPTER 7

1 Bob Chapman, interview, April 25, 2013.
2 Scott Leibs, "Putting People Before the Bottom Line (and Still Making Money)," Inc, May 2014, http://www.inc.com/audacious-companies/scott-leibs/barry-wehmiller.html.
3 Chapman, interview, April 25, 2013.
4 Leibs, "Putting People."
5 http://www.shrm.org/legalissues/stateandlocalresources/stateand localstatutesandregulations/documents/12-0537 2012 jobsatisfaction _fnl_online.pdf.
6 Sigal Barsade and Olivia (Mandy) O'Neill, "Employees Who Feel Love Perform Better," Harvard Business Review, January 13, 2014.
7 T. Rath, Vital Friends: The People You Can't Afford to Live Without (New York: Gallup Press, 2006).
8 K. Nowack and P. J. Zak, "The Neuroscience of Building High Performance Trust Cultures," Talent Magazine, in press.
9 P. J. Zak, Moral Molecule: The Source of Love and Prosperity (New York: Dutton 2012).
10 http://www.fastcompany.com/3008976/leadership-now/jerry-seinfeld-on-the-perfection-of-the-coffee-meeting.
11 P. J. Kolesar, "Vision, values, milestones: Paul O'Neill starts total quality at Alcoa," California Management Review, 35 no. 3, (1993): 133–165.
12 Those numbers are per 200,000 work hours," http://emeetingplace.com/safetyblog/2008/06/05/workplace-safety-a-prespective-from-paul-oneill/Data: from 1.86 per 100 workers in 1987 to 0.14 per 100 workers in 2001.
13 http://www.archcoal.com/aboutus/safety.aspx.
14 Onwuham C. Akpa interview with author, Feburary 15, 2015.
15 http://www.medscape.com/features/slideshow/lifestyle/2013/public?src=soc_tw_lifcst.
16 https://www.advisory.com/daily-briefing/2013/12/03/when-cleveland-clinic-staff-are-troubled-they-file-code-lavender.
17 http://experiahealthblog.com/category/code-lavender/.
18 Saima Naeem and Asad Zaman, "For Love or Money? Motivating Workers," Pakistan Institute of Development Economics Working Paper (2013): 90.
19 Zak, Moral Molecule.
20 http://www.tatasteel.com/about-us/heritage/century-of-trust.asp21.

https://www.equitymaster.com/help/press-releases/Tata-voted-the-Most-Trustworthy-Corporate-Group.html.

22 Frauke Rost, interview with the author, April 2015, Claremont, CA.

23 Adam Grant, *Give and Take: Why Helping Others Drives our Success.* (New York: Penguin, 2013).

24 https://hbr.org/2013/12/how-google-sold-its-engineers-on-management.

25 Daina Beth Solomon, "Amazon Report Sparks Debate," *Los Angeles Times,* August 18, 2015, C3.

26 Teresa Amabile, Colin M. Fisher, and Julianna Pillemer, "IDEO's Culture of Helping," *Harvard Business Review,* January 2014.

27 http://www.ted.com/talks/tim_brown_on_creativity_and_play#t-216303.

28 D. H. Thom and B. Campbell, "Patient-Physician Trust: An Exploratory Study," *Journal of Family Practice* 44, no. 2 (1997): 169–177.

29 H. Riess, J. M. Kelley, R. W. Bailey, E. J. Dunn, and M. Phillips, "Empathy Training for Resident Physicians: A Randomized Controlled Trial of a Neuroscience-Informed Curriculum," *Journal of General Internal Medicine* 27, no. 10 (2012):1280–1286; Sandra G. Boodman, "How to Teach Doctors Empathy," *Atlantic,* March 15, 2015, http://www.theatlantic.com/health/archive/2015/03/how-to-teach-doctors-empathy/387784/.

30 "2015 Employee Benefits: An Overview of Employee Benefits Offerings in the U.S. Society for Human Resource Management," 2015. https://www.shrm.org/hr-today/trends-and-forecasting/research-and-surveys/Documents/2015-Employee-Benefits.pdf.

31 http://www.aboutmcdonalds.com/mcd/corporate_careers/benefits/highlights_of_what_we_offer/balance_work_and_life.html.

32 John Waggoner, "Morningstar's Mansueto: Quiet Guide, Driving Force," *USA Today,* June 27, 2013, 3B.

33 Keith Richards and James Fox, *Life,* (New York: Back Bay Books, 2011).

34 Andrew Park, "What You Don't Know About Dell," *Businessweek,* November 2, 2003 http://www.businessweek.com/stories/2003-11-02/what-you-dont-know-about-dell.

35 http://www.druckerinstitute.com/2014/01/what-peter-drucker-would-be-reading-87/.

36 Tim Worstall, "Apple's Tim Cook Voluntarily Forgoes $75 Million Payout," Forbes.com, June 22, 2013 http://www.forbes.com/sites/

timworstall/2012/05/25/apples-tim-cook-voluntarily-forgoes-75-million-payout/.

37 Jeff Vrabel, "Why Are There So Many Bad Bosses? Some People Are Natural-Born Leaders. Others Are Cruel, Inhuman Monsters," *Success*, Towers Watson Global Workforce Study, 2012.

38 http://www.futureofbusinessandtech.com/education-and-careers/business-guru-jim-goodnights-innovative-approach-to-leadership.

39 http://blogs.sas.com/content/sastraining/2011/12/07/mmm-dr-g-and-the-mms/.

40 Wayne Cascio, John Boudreau, Alison Davis, Jane Shannon, and David Russo, *HR Strategies for Employee Engagement (Collection)*. (Upper Saddle River, NJ: FT Press, 2011).

41 James M. Kouzes, and Barry Z. Posner. *The Truth About Leadership: The No-Fads, heart-of-the-Matter Facts You Need to Know*. (New York: John Wiley & Sons, 2010).

42 Bock, *Work Rules!*

43 T. Louie, Lululemon Athletica: Organizational Analysis Using The Ofactor Framework. PSYCH350ee 2015 final project, Claremont Graduate University.

44 Work with Google. Nov 10, 2014, https://www.youtube.com/watch?v=DGqzRUfH52o.

45 Gregory G. Hennessy, "An Exploration of the Relationship Between Organizational Culture and Daily Experience" (master's thesis, Claremont Graduate University, May 2015).

46 "Sales Force Effectiveness: A 'Street Level' View Research Report," Forum Corporation. 2016. http://www.forum.com/wp-content/uploads/2016/03/Sales-Force-Effectiveness-A-Street-Level-View.pdf.

47 Joshua Freedman, "The Business Case for Emotional Intelligence," Six Seconds, 2016, http://www.6seconds.org/case/business-case-ebook/.

48 Zak, *Moral Molecule*; H. Y. Weng, A. S. Fox, A. J. Shackman, D. E. Stodola, J. Z. Caldwell, M. C. Olson, and R. J. Davidson, "Compassion Training Alters Altruism and Neural Responses to Suffering," *Psychological Science* 24, no. 7 (2013): 1171–1180.

49 http://www.bloomberg.com/bw/magazine/content/10_38/b4195058423479.htm#p5.

50 P. F. Drucker, "They're Not Employees, They're People," *Harvard Business Review*, 80 no. 2, 70–7.

51 Gretchen Spreitzer and Christine Porath, "Creating Sustainable Performance," *Harvard Business Review*, January–February 2012.

CHAPTER 8

1 Colman Lydon, "Why Should Employers Invest in Continuous Learning?," Modern Workforce, December 24, 2014, https://www.geteverwise.com/talent-development/why-should-employers-invest-in-continuous-learning/.

2 Josh Bersin, "The Year of the Employee: Predictions For Talent, Leadership, And HR Technology," Forbes, December 19, 2014.

3 Spherion Staffing Services, "Skills Gap, Turnover Are Top Talent Concerns," Emerging Workforce Study, conducted by Harris Poll, 2015, http://www.shrm.org/hrdisciplines/staffingmanagement/articles/.

4 Accenture, US College Graduate Employment Study, 2015.

5 Robert Kegan et al. "Making Business Personal." Harvard Business Review 92 no. 4 (2014): 44–52.

6 Deloitte, "Global Human Capital Trends 2015: Leading in the New World of Work," Deloitte University Press, http://www2.deloitte.com/content/dam/Deloitte/at/Documents/human-capital/hc-trends-2015.pdf.

7 Laurie Miller, "ASTD 2012 State of the Industry Report: Organizations Continue to Invest in Workplace Learning," TD Magazine. November 8, 2012, https://www.td.org/Publications/Magazines/TD/TD-Archive/2012/11/ASTD-2012-State-of-the-Industry-Report.

8 Carol D. Ryff and Corey Lee M. Keyes. "The structure of Psychological Well-Being Revisited." Journal of Personality and Social Psychology 69 no. 4 (1995): 719–727.

9 http://www.dailymail.co.uk/news/article-3061354/Having-challenging-job-prevent-dementia-helps-brain-active-slows-rate-decline-memory-thinking-study-says.html; http://www.nytimes.com/2012/04/22/magazine/how-exercise-could-lead-to-a-better-brain.html.

10 Philip Kotler, "Why Investing in Workers Makes Companies Richer," Business Insider, April 13, 2015.

11 Steven E. Scullen, Michael K. Mount, and Maynard Goff, "Understanding the Latent Structure of Job Performance Ratings." Journal of Applied Psychology 85 no. 6 (2000): 956.; James K. Harter, Frank L. Schmidt, and Theodore L. Hayes., "Business-Unit-Level Relationship Between Employee Satisfaction, Employee Engagement, and Business Outcomes: A Meta-analysis." Journal of Applied Psychology 87 no. 2 (2002): 268.

12   Matthew Klein (L&D Business Partner, People Operations), interview with the author, February 25, 2015, Mountain View, CA.

13   Marcus Buckingham and Ashley Goodall, "Reinventing Performance Management," *Harvard Business Review,* April 2015.

14   http://www.wsj.com/articles/SB10001424052702303410404577466 852658514144.

15   Laszlo Bock, *Work Rules! Insights from Inside Google That Will Transform How You Live and Lead* (New York: Twelve, 2015).

16   C. Peterson, *A Primer in Positive Psychology* (Oxford: Oxford University Press, 2006).

17   Chip Conley, *Peak: How Great Companies Get Their Mojo from Maslow,* (New York: John Wiley & Sons, 2007).

18   http://www.businessweek.com/managing/content/apr2011/ ca2011046_719401.htm.

19   T. Brower, *Bring Work to Life by Bringing Life to Work: A Guide for Leaders and Organizations,* (New York: Routledge 2014).

20   Beth Kowitt and Colleen Leahey, "Lululemon: In an Uncomfortable Position" *Fortune,* August 29, 2013, http://fortune.com/2013/08/29/ lululemon-in-an-uncomfortable-position/.

21   Max Nisen, "How Facebook's Fancy New York Office Explains Its Management Philosophy," *Quartz,* July 29, 2014, http://qz. com/229542/facebook-office/.

22   http://talent.linkedin.com/blog/index.php/2014/11/why-did-ditch- its-job-postings-and-is-the-strategy-working.

23   Melissa Reiff (The Container Store president), interview with the author, June 29, 2011, Dallas, TX.

24   http://online.wsj.com/news/articles/SB10001424052702303 912104575164573823418844?http://clomedia.com/articles/viewups -promoting-learning.

25   Amanda MacMillian, "Insomnia Costs U.S. $63 Billion Annually in Lost Productivity," CNN, September 1, 2011, http://www.cnn. com/2011/09/01/health/insomnia-cost-productivity/.

26   Tom Stafford, "How Sleep Makes You More Creative," BBC online, December 5, 2013, http://www.bbc.com/future/story/20131205- how-sleep-makes-you-more-creative.

27   Joe Pinsker, "Corporations' Newest Productivity Hack: Meditation," *Atlantic,* March 19, 2015.

28   Rob Quinn, "Bad News for Those Who Work More Than 55 Hours a Week," Fox News, August 20, 2015.

29   Keith Ferrazzi, "7 Ways to Improve Employee Development Programs," *Harvard Business Review,* July 31, 2015, https://hbr.

org/2015/07/7-ways-to-improve-employee-development-programs; "The Human Era @ Work: Findings from The Energy Project and Harvard Business Review, 2014," http://uli.org/wp-content/uploads/ULI-Documents/The-Human-Era-at-Work.pdf.

30 http://www.nytimes.com/2014/06/01/opinion/sunday/why-you-hate-work.html?_r=0.

31 Stephanie Kirchgaessner, "Pope Francis Makes Scathing Critique of Vatican Officials in Curia Speech," *Guardian*, December 22, 2014, http://www.theguardian.com/world/2014/dec/22/pope-francis-scathing-critique-vatican-officials-curia-speech.

32 http://www.theatlantic.com/business/archive/2015/06/all-the-happy-workers/394907/; http://www.businessfightsaids.org/news/newsletters/2012/july/case-study-of-the-month-unilever/.

33 R. Feinzeig, "Companies Try 'Firm 40' Workweeks," *Wall Street Journal*, October 14, 2015.

34 Cathleen Benko and Anne Weisberg "The Journey Toward a Lattice Organization," HBR Press Book Chapter #: 3885BC-PDF-ENG, September 20, 2007, https://hbr.org/product/the-journey-toward-a-lattice-organization-implementing-the-principles-of-mass-career-customization/3885BC-PDF-ENG ; Jeffrey Pfeffer, *SAS Institute: The Decision to Go Public*, (Stanford Graduate School of Business, 2000).

35 J. Pfeffer, "Kent Thiry and DaVita: Leadership Challenges in Building and Growing a Great Company.". Stanford Graduate School of Business Case OB-64, February 23, 2006.

36 Decurion Corp., 2016, http://www.decurion.com/dec/.

CHAPTER 9

1 Randall Beck and Jim Harter, "Managers Account for 70% of Variance in Employee Engagement," *Gallup Business Journal*, April 21, 2015, http://www.gallup.com/businessjournal/182792/managers-account-variance-employee-engagement.aspx.

2 https://hbr.org/2015/05/how-to-earn-respect-as-a-leader.

3 http://www.nytimes.com/2016/02/28/magazine/what-google-learned-from-its-quest-to-build-the-perfect-team.html.

4 P. J. Zak, *The Moral Molecule: The Source of Love and Prosperity*. (New York: Dutton, 2012).

5 Adam Bryant, "Steven Mollenkopf of Qualcomm: If You Don't Know, Just Say So," *New York Times*, September 20, 2014.

6   http://gladwell.com/blink/why-do-we-love-tall-men/.

7   Steven Berglas, "The Entrepreneurial Ego: Pratfalls. A Clinical Psychologist Explains Why It's Good for Every Leader to Stumble Through Pratfalls," Inc., September 1, 1996, http://www.inc.com/magazine/19960901/1796.html.

8   E. Aronson, B. Willerman, and J. Floyd, "The Effect of a Pratfall on Increasing Interpersonal Attractiveness," *Psychonomic Science* 4 (1966): 227–228.

9   http://www.brainyquote.com/quotes/keywords/admit.html.

10 Nate Boaz and Erica Ariel Fox, "Change Leader, Change Thyself," *McKinsey Quarterly*, March 2014.

11 Alexandra Wilson Pecci, "Physician Burnout Heavily Influenced by Leadership Behaviors," HealthLeaders Media, April 28, 2015.

12 http://mashable.com/2014/10/30/tim-cook-industry-reactions/.

13 http://www.netpromotersystemblog.com/2016/04/25/set-perfection-as-the-goal-leadership-lessons-from-former-vanguard-ceo-jack-brennan/.

14 Lauren Weber, "Changing Corporate Culture Is Hard: Here's How Lenovo Did It," *Wall Street Journal*, August 25, 2014.

15 Andrew Bary, "World's Best CEOs," *Barron's*, March 25, 2013. http://www.barrons.com/articles/SB50001424052748704836204578362542870655514.

16 Kevin Freiberg, and Jackie Freiberg, "Nuts!: Southwest Airlines' crazy recipe for business and personal success," (New York: Broadway, 1996).

17 Abby Ohlheiser, "Today's Lunch Special in the Vatican Cafeteria: Pope Francis!," *Washington Post*, July 25, 2014.

18 https://www.linkedin.com/pulse/i-were-22-never-cut-corners-integrity-everything-lowell-mcadam.

19 Anita E. Kelly, "Study: Telling the Truth May Actually Improve Your Health," *Psychology Today Blogs*, Aug 9, 2014, https://www.psychologytoday.com/blog/insight/201408/study-telling-the-truth-may-actually-improve-your-health.

20 http://knowledge.wharton.upenn.edu/article/why-strong-leadership-is-all-about-trust.

21 https://hbr.org/2015/05/the-leadership-behavior-thats-most-important-to-employees.

22 Melissa Korn and Rachel Feintzeig, "Is the Hard-Nosed Boss Obsolete?," *Wall Street Journal*, May 22, 2014.

23 https://www.washingtonpost.com/news/on-leadership/wp/2013/09/19/whats-the-right-ratio-for-ceo-to-worker-pay/.

24 https://www.glassdoor.com/research/ceo-pay-ratio/.

25 Jena McGregor, "On Leadership: Costco Chief Executive Jim Sinegal," *Washington Post*, September 10, 2011. https://www.washingtonpost. com/business/on-leadership-costco-chief-executive-jim-sinegal/ 2011/09/07/gIQAQ59SIK_story.html.

26 Chip Conley, *Peak: How Great Companies Get Their Mojo from Maslow*, (New York: John Wiley & Sons, 2007), 62.

27 Susan Adams, "The Highest-Paid CEOs Are the Worst Performers, New Study Says," *Forbes*, June 6, 2014.

28 Ketchum, "Leadership Communication Monitor," https://www. ketchum.com/2015-leadership-communication-monitor.

29 Robert L. Gandt, *Skygods: The Fall of Pan Am* (New York: William Morrow & Company, 1995).

30 Transport Canada, *Human Factors for Aviation—Advanced Handbook*, TP 12864 (E), 93–94.

31 Robert K. Greenleaf and Larry C. Spears, *Servant Leadership: A Journey into the Nature of Legitimate Power and Greatness.* (Mahwah, NJ: Paulist Press, 2002); Blanchard, Ken, and Phil Hodges. *Servant Leader* (Nashville, TN: Thomas Nelson, 2003).

32 Sendjaya, Sen, and Andre Pekerti. "Servant Leadership as Antecedent of Trust in Organizations." *Leadership & Organization Development Journal* 31 no. 7 (2010): 643–663.

33 Kevin Kruse, "100 Best Quotes On Leadership," *Forbes*, October 16, 2012.

CHAPTER 10

1 http://www.forbes.com/sites/stevedenning/2013/06/26/the-origin- of-the-worlds-dumbest-idea-milton-friedman/#19002a5b214c.

2 Steve Denning, "The Origin of 'The World's Dumbest Idea': Milton Friedman," *Forbes*, June 26, 2013, http://www.forbes.com/sites/steve denning/2013/06/26/the-origin-of-the-worlds-dumbest-idea- milton-friedman/#719c2880214c.

3 Ibid.

4 P. J. Zak, *The Moral Molecule: The Source of Love and Prosperity.* (New York: Dutton, 2012).

5 P. E. Schmuck and K. M. Sheldon, *Life Goals and Well-Being: Towards a Positive Psychology of Human Striving* (Boston: Hogrefe & Huber, 2001).

6 https://www.youtube.com/watch?v=tnlNUZqFzgY.

7   V. E. Frankl, "Man's search for meaning," (New York: Simon and Schuster, 1985).

8   Peter Drucker, *The Practice of Management,* (New York: Harper, 1954): 327.

9   Andreas Widmer, *The Pope & the CEO: John Paul II's Leadership Lessons to a Young Swiss Guard* (Steubenville, OH: Emmaus Road Publishing, 2011).

10 Deloitte Development LLC, *Culture of Purpose: A Business Imperative, 2013 Core Beliefs & Culture Survey, 2013.*

11 Personal interview, San Francisco, CA Feb 25, 2015.

12 J. A. Barraza, V. Alexander, L. E. Beavin, E. T. Terris, and P. J. Zak, "The Heart of the Story: Peripheral Physiology During Narrative Exposure Predicts Charitable Giving," *Biological Psychology* 105 (2015): 138–143.

13 James C. Collins and Jerry I. Porras, "Building Your Company's Vision," *Harvard Business Review, October 1, 1996, 65.*

14 Paul J. Zak, "Why Inspiring Stories Make Us React: The Neuroscience of Narrative." *Cerebrum: The Dana Forum on Brain Science.* vol. 2015, Dana Foundation, 2015.

15 Doug Rauch (Trader Joe's former CEO), interview with the author, 2012, Claremont, CA.

16 Paul Zak, "Why Your Brain Loves Good Storytelling." *Harvard Business Review,* October 28, 2014, https://hbr.org/2014/10/why-your-brain-loves-good-storytelling.

17 Adam Grant, *Give and Take: Why Helping Others Drives Our Success.* (New York: Penguin, 2013).

18 http://www.ocregister.com/articles/disney-707478-disneyland-year.html.

19 Zak, *Moral Molecule.*

20 http://www.sfgate.com/news/article/Apple-layoffs-Painful-but-necessary-3130407.php, and B. Schlender, *Becoming Steve Jobs.*

21 Verne Harnish, "5 Ways to Get More from Your PR Efforts," *Fortune,* March 1, 2015, 38.

22 Maritz Global Events, http://www.maritzglobalevents.com/About-Us/Giving-Back.

23 Ty Montague, "The Rise of Storydoing: Inside the Staggering Success of Toms Shoes," Fast Company, August 5, 2013, http://www.fastcompany.com/3015209/leadership-now/the-rise-of-storydoing-inside-the-staggering-success-of-toms-shoes.

24 T. Montague, *True Story: How to Combine Story and Action to Transform Your Business* (Cambridge: Harvard Business Review Press, 2013).

25   http://www.storydoing.com/conversation.

26   https://hbr.org/product/monsanto-helping-farmers-feed-the-world/510025-PDF-ENG.

27   Bruce N. Pfau, "How an Accounting Firm Convinced Its Employees They Could Change the World," *Harvard Business Review,* October 6, 2015.

28   Robert Hackett, "KPMG's Viral Morale Meme," *Fortune*, February 19, 2015.

29   Angela Jeffs, "Calling on the Right Brain for Creative Strategy," *Japan Times*, December 9, 2006, http://www.japantimes.co.jp/community/2006/12/09/general/calling-on-the-right-brain-for-creative-strategy/#.V8MkN1fw_n8.

30   "Richard Branson on Why Making Employees Happy Pays Off," *Entrepreneur,* April 7, 2014.

31   S. M. Schaefer, J. M. Boylan, C. M. Van Reekum, et al., "Purpose in Life Predicts Better Emotional Recovery from Negative Stimuli," *PloS one*, 8 no. 11 (2013), e80329.

32   Emily Esfahani Smith, "There's More to Life Than Being Happy," *Atlantic*, January 9, 2013.

33   J. L. Brown, D. Sheffield, M. R. Leary, and M. E. Robinson, "Social Support and Experimental Pain," *Psychosomatic Medicine* 65, no. 2 (2003): 276–283.

34   Laszlo Bock, *Work Rules! Insights from Inside Google That Will Transform How You Live and Lead* (New York: Twelve, 2015).

35   https://workplacedemocracy.com/tag/davita/.

36   Ashoka, "To Win the War for Talent, Give Them Purpose, Not Just a Paycheck," *Forbes,* September 17, 2014.

37   http://www.theguardian.com/sustainable-business/2015/jan/23/benefit-corporations-bcorps-business-social-responsibility.

38   Peter F. Drucker, "What Business Can Learn from Nonprofits, *Harvard Business Review,* July–August 1989.

39   Peter F. Drucker, *The Age of Discontinuity* (New York: HarperCollins Publishers, 1969).

40   Cosette Cornelis, Elizabeth T. Terris, Mitchell J. Neubert, et al., "Social Purpose Increases Direct-to-Borrower Microfinance Investments," manuscript, Center for Neuroeconomics Studies, Claremont Graduate University.

41   Alexander and Zak, "How Open Office Design Affects Teamwork: A Neurophysiological Field Study," manuscript in review.

42   Correlation coefficent $r = .77 > 0$ at $p = .00001$.

43   Rajendra Sisodia, Jagdish N. Sheth, and David Wolfe, *Firms of*

Endearment: How World-Class Companies Profit from Passion and Purpose (Upper Saddle River, NJ: FT Press 2007), 14.

44 Jim Stengel, "Grow: How Ideals Power Growth and Profit at the World's Greatest Companies," (New York: Crown Business, 2011).

45 D. S. Yeager, M. D. Henderson, D. Paunesku, et al., "Boring But Important: A Self-Transcendent Purpose for Learning Fosters Academic Self-Regulation," *Journal of Personality and Social Psychology*, 107 no. 4 (2014): 559.

46 Veronika Alexander, Jesse R. Kluver, and Paul J. Zak, "Neurophysiology of Organizational Culture at a Major Retailer," manuscript, Center for Neuroeconomics Studies, Claremont Graduate University, 2014.

47 J. Carpenter and E. Gong, "Motivating Agents: How Much Does the Mission Matter?" *Journal of Labor Economics*, 34 no. 1 (2016): 211–236.

48 http://www.goodreads.com/quotes/772887-the-only-way-to-do-great-work-is-to-love.

49 http://www.theatlantic.com/magazine/archive/2016/04/quit-your-job/471501/.

CHAPTER 11

1 Data from Veronika Alexander, Jesse R. Kluver, and Paul J. Zak, "Neurophysiology of Organizational Culture at a Major Retailer, " manuscript, Center for Neuroeconomics Studies, Claremont Graduate University, 2014.

2 Alexander and Zak, "How Open Office Design Affects Teamwork: A Neurophysiological Field Study," manuscript in review.

3 The correlation $r = 0.26$ is statistically significant at $p > .01$.

4 We copied the apple-peeler idea from my friend and colleague Panagiotis Mitkidis at Aarhus University. It was first used in Panagiotis Mitkidis, Michael Bang Petersen, Paul J. Zak et al., "Alienation from: A Lack of Shared Knowledge Decreases Cooperativen Cooperation ess Towards Second and Third Parties," manuscript in review.

5 Oasis Kodila-Tedika and Julius Agbor Agbor, "Does Trust Matter for Entrepreneurship: Evidence from a Cross-Section of Countries," Munich Personal RePEc Archive, University of Kinshasa, Brookings Institution, Stellenbosch University, October 29, 2012, http://mpra.ub.uni-muenchen. de/46306/8/MPRA_paper_46306.pdf.

6 T. M. Amabile, S. G. Barsade, J. S. Mueller, and B. M. Staw, "Affect and Creativity at Work," *Administrative Science Quarterly*, 50 (2005): 367–403.

7   Shana Lynch, "Why Your Workplace Might Be Killing You," Stanford Business Insights, February 23, 2015.

8   The correlation $r = 0.23$ is statistically significant at $p = .05$.

9   R. Z. Goetzel et al., "Health, Absence, Disability, and Presenteeism Cost Estimates of Certain Physical and Mental Health Conditions Affecting U.S. Employers," *Journal of Occupational and Environmental Medicine* 46 (April 2004): 398–412.

10 http://www.forbes.com/sites/brucejapsen/2012/09/12/u-s-workforce-illness-costs-576b-annually-from-sick-days-to-workers-compensation/#efce5a37256f.

11 http://kff.org/health-costs/report/2015-employer-health-benefits-survey/.

12 https://osha.europa.eu/en/tools-and-publications/publications/literature_reviews/calculating-the-cost-of-work-related-stress-and-psychosocial-risks; https://www.uml.edu/Research/Centers/CPH-NEW/stress-at-work/financial-costs.aspx; https://www.gsb.stanford.edu/insights/why-your-workplace-might-be-killing-you.

13 Using a 6 percent discount rate.

14 R. Goffee, and G. Jones, "Creating the best workplace on earth," *Harvard Business Review*, 91 no. 5 (2013): 98–106.

15 http://intelispend.com/blog/23-employee-motivation-statistics-to-silence-naysayers.

16 A. Edmans, "Does the Stock Market Fully Value Intangibles? Employee Satisfaction and Equity Prices," *Journal of Financial Economics* 101 (2011): 621–640.

Index